The Heart's Gift

Jodi Davis

Beaver's Pond Press, Inc.
Edina, Minnesota

This is a true story, however, some of the names have been changed to protect the privacy of certain individuals.

ISBN 1-59298-006-6

Library of Congress Catalog Number: 2003103782

Book design and typesetting: Mori Studio
Cover design: Mori Studio

Printed in the United States of America

First Printing: April 2003

06 05 04 03 02   6 5 4 3 2 1

Beaver's Pond Press, Inc.   7104 Ohms Lane Suite 216
Edina, MN 55439
(952) 829-8818
www.BeaversPondPress.com

To order, visit *BookHouseFulfillment.com* or call
1-800-901-3480. Reseller discounts available.

Dedication

To my children—my blessings,
each of whom have gifts of their own.

JD, a woman with an inner beauty and a deep capacity to love.
Your children will be blessed with an exceptional mother.

My son, words do not describe our bond.
Your innate gifts, together with your life experiences, have
created a man rich in passion, integrity, character and love.
Hold your head high as you continue on your path.

And Boo, I couldn't imagine life without you.
Your astonishing beauty is complemented by
so many natural talents. Reach for the stars—
you have the greatest chance in the
Universe to achieve your dreams.

✆ ACKNOWLEDGEMENTS

It is with deep appreciation that I acknowledge my family, beginning with my mother, who from the earliest days encouraged me to write creatively and explore my passion. My brother, who encouraged me to think for myself and to rely on my own innate capabilities when I plunged forth into independence. Babe, a special mother, who supported my life as a single woman—your compliments were high praise and greatly appreciated. Jenny, who lived all of this with me, and who lovingly and unselfishly helped me to accomplish my goals. Beth, who missed knowing her sister, but whose own existence was the greatest gift of all. And Tim, your love for Jill and for me is indescribable. Your role as my special editor was invaluable and beautifully executed.

Three friends, whose literary expertise provided me with quality feedback, encouragement, and direction—Thank you for listening, editing, and adding commas: Carolyn Riley, the quintessential "Comma Queen"; Kathy Jerue, a woman whose eyes smiled approval and excitement for my work; and Stephanie Rowh, as in "wow," a woman warrior, who pushed me toward my goal in the midst of the corporate adversity we shared.

Deb Cloud, thank you for loving Jill as you did and for sharing my memories. I so appreciated your willingness to critique my story and refine the medical descriptions so that they accurately reflect her care. Jill was blessed with the gift of you.

Milt Adams, of Beavers Pond Press—there would be no book without you. Thank you for embracing me as a BPP author and for having confidence in my ability. When I saw your Website description of the "Mentoring and Coaching Publisher," I knew you were the publishing world's gift to me.

Cindy Rogers, my editor: you gave wings to my words. Your insightful literary talent infused me with confidence, and my heart soared as I clarified, strengthened, and revised my original work. Your encouragement to think of this process as "polishing the gem" allowed me to bring forth a final product that radiated from your editorial brilliance.

Jack and Jaana, from Mori Studio—your ability to turn my written words into a magnificent final product truly captured the essence of my heart. As professionals, your guidance was superb! As individuals, your compassion for my story was greatly appreciated.

Nancy Haskin—thank you for supporting my love of Children's for the past twenty years. I admire your professional success and grace as a leader. Steve Lundin, for showing me in graduate school that I could achieve my dreams, and for reappearing in my life to express encouragement and share memories of our daughters. Sandy Swanson, for your willingness to read my memoir without knowing me and for embracing my story as the beginning of our friendship. Todd Blackwell, whose own success speaks to me of how intellect, competence and perseverance, can bring an individual to the pinnacle of success even amidst adversity.

Lastly I would like to acknowledge the generous permission granted by:

- ⚭ Diane Von Arx, for the poem "Anticipation," a gift I will always treasure;

- ⚭ Stan Tillotson, for the photograph of my beloved statue found at Stan's Porcelain Website www.stan.tillotson.com;

- ⚭ Royal Scandinavia, USA, for the Royal Copenhagen "Come to Mom" image that captured the heart and soul of my daughter's relationship with me.

Anticipation

Wouldn't it be nice
if we would treat each experience
with the same sensitivity and
appreciation as we treat the
memories of that experience.

Too often an occasion is
not nearly as enjoyable as we hoped
it would be, nor as precious as we
remember it to be, simply because
we do not enjoy it to the fullest
while it is ours.

April 3, 2002

My dearest Jill:

Today is your twenty-first birthday. The age of emancipation. Twenty-one marks the true commencement of adulthood and the dawn of womanhood for a young female. Twenty-one is generally an age when the future stands before us as a pure canvas waiting to be painted with the vibrant colors of one's life experiences. Usually it all lies ahead.

But, my darling Jill, your birthday holds a very different meaning for me. These twenty-one years since your birth have been a lifetime unto themselves. The years since you were born have unfolded into a journey of remarkable growth, self-discovery, passionate learning, and love. There has been exceptional achievement and true metamorphosis.

Your twenty-first birthday brings me full circle to an end of a story rather than to the cusp of a new one. This is my story, Jill. Your birth and life helped create my own life. I am firmly convinced that giving birth to you, caring for you, and loving you as I did, cast me on a new path. It was through knowing you that life was breathed into my own existence. Your birth was the catalyst that spawned my own development and independence.

The journals and letters I have kept over the past twenty-one years chronicle lessons of intimacy, career exploration, transformation, empowerment, and love...all difficult assignments set before an already grown woman to embrace and explore. The journey has been recorded as if I could pass it back to you, my daughter, to teach you the normal lessons of life and of growing up.

Whenever I have told your story it has become inextricably linked with mine. I feel a deep sense of gratitude each time I speak of the unconditional love and memories of you. The quicksand of time has pulled most of the pain and sadness far from my consciousness. What remains, instead, is the sense of joy that your life has had a true purpose—a significance more powerful than most. Jill, I am so grateful for the gift of you.

Love,
Mom

∽ PART I ∾

ᨓ AUGUST 1, 1980

Today is my ninth wedding anniversary. It seems an appropriate day to begin this diary. I am pregnant. This is my third pregnancy, and if it progresses without incident, I will deliver my third child in late March or early April. I speak with reserved excitement, because once again I am cramping and spotting with this pregnancy—which places me in the high-risk category. High risk for miscarriage.

Actually I am optimistic that everything will go okay, just as it did for my first two babies. Nevertheless, my doctor warned me yesterday about the risks associated with pregnancies when there is bleeding. In any case, this is still an important time in my life and I want to record everything to save the memories.

It is hard to believe that I am pregnant as I write this. Aside from the constant nausea and overwhelming sleepiness that I feel every afternoon, I can usually forget that I am pregnant. In fact, to date, we have told no one. My pregnancy has been mostly my secret for some time now.

I most likely conceived around the sixth of July. My due date should be about March 27, 1981. This pregnancy is four years after my last, and it is interesting to see how medical technology has improved. This time I was able to have a test called the "serum pregnancy" test, which identifies the pregnancy hormone HCG in the blood as early as ten days after conception. I took a serum test on July 16 and it was negative. Of course, I was disappointed since I was sure I was pregnant. I continued to believe my symptoms meant something significant. Sure enough, when I repeated the test several days later, the results were finally positive.

I have been playing the analytical numbers game since I found out. If I conceived on the thirteenth or fourteenth day of the month, then the baby will be born on or around my due date of March 27. But since both my other children were delivered "late" and since I "flunked" my first pregnancy test, then most likely I conceived later and the baby will come sometime in the first week of April. It's fun to speculate.

If I had to guess right now, I would say I am pregnant with another girl. No special reason for thinking that way, just maternal instinct. I associate my minimal weight gain with having a girl and I "feel" small like I did with my first pregnancy when my daughter, Alicia, was born. With three children, another girl would mean my son, Anthony, a middle child, would be the singular boy, thus giving him some special place in the family. Certainly at this point the planning is out of my control. It's all speculation.

⌒ AUGUST 22, 1980

It's been three weeks since I began this diary and several things have happened. My negative feelings about a problem with this pregnancy have dissipated. Many of my fears were lodged deep in a premonition that I was getting sick. I had a viral flu, with a fever of 101°, for almost two weeks. I sat curled up on my den sofa, just staring out the window at the summer sky. Tears trickled down my checks, and I hugged my knees close into my body in an effort to comfort my achy emptiness. I have no recollection of the weather, or the events of those days. I only remember a monotonous melancholy that draped my spirits in darkness. I can't even tell you if the sun was shining or if it was warm outside. All that seemed to matter was that I felt sick. For a while, I was certain that something was going to be wrong with the baby. I called my doctor to express my fears.

At times, I didn't even feel pregnant. It was too early to feel signs of life, but I so wanted to feel something other than illness. I even made my doctor give me another pregnancy test to reassure myself that I was, in fact, still pregnant. Once I got over the flu virus, my mood improved and I emerged from the gloom feeling nauseated and pregnant again.

I will begin my third month in five days, but still no weight gain. I have a great deal of nausea, although my worst morning sickness comes between one and three o'clock in the morning. I am taking "anti-nausea" pills (benedectine), and while I haven't really gained weight, I do feel bloated and bigger, especially right after I eat and at night. Speaking of night, I'm often sleepy but I don't nap regularly. That's probably due to the two active toddlers, Alicia (Ali), age 6, and Anthony (Tony), age 3, who are running around during the day. But they happen to be asleep right now, so I think I will try for a quick "Mommy nap."

∞ SEPTEMBER 4, 1980

Today was the nicest day of my pregnancy so far. The main reason is related to the marvels of modern medicine. It began last Friday when I saw my doctor for the two-month checkup. Everything looked good, but just to be sure, he ordered a special test—an ultrasound.

The ultrasound machine scans the abdomen and picks up high frequency sound waves and converts them to pictures on a screen. Subsequently, the pictures land on film for a doctor's viewing and diagnosis. The main purpose of the test is to check for a fetal heartbeat and movement. The radiologist can also give a basic diagnosis of approximate age of the fetus to see if it coincides with the due date.

My ultrasound was fantastic! I actually saw a tiny, tiny baby inside of me and I watched a minute heart beating very, very fast! Getting ready for the test is another story in itself. Painfully funny, actually.

It's quite important for the pregnant woman to drink at least six glasses of water at least one hour before she is to have the test, to help push the uterus (which lies above the bladder) way up into the abdomen. A completely full bladder will accomplish this successfully. The reason for pushing the uterus up is to create a clearer image and picture on film.

I always do what I am told. This time, I followed instructions so well that I drank six very full glasses of water long before the hour prior to my ultrasound. I thought I was going to either scream or burst. By 12:10 P.M., I called the hospital to ask if I could come in early because I was beginning to experience pain. They said okay.

I went alone and the driving was almost unbearable. Moving my foot from the accelerator to the brake moved my already uncomfortable bladder into a state of misery. By the time I got to the registration department, I couldn't sit down and I pleaded with them to rush me through. They did and I was on my way to the radiology department, which of course was the very last door down a very long hall. When I got there, I was sure my bladder was going to rupture. Unfortunately, the technician assigned to my ultrasound was out to lunch! I almost started to cry. Finally, they let me go to the bathroom (just a little) but the relief was short-lived and I was still miserably uncomfortable. I would have laughed at the comedic situation, except that I was afraid I would wet my pants!

Finally, the technician returned from lunch and my ultrasound was underway. The test itself was awesome! I didn't understand most of what I saw, but I did see a miniature baby structure with an actual pulselike dot that beat quite fast. The doctor who saw me at the end of the scanning said he was watching my heart beating and he could also see the baby's heart. He said the baby's heart was beating five times faster than mine. He also said the heart looked like the right size for a nine-to-eleven week pregnancy. It has been eleven weeks since my last period and approximately nine weeks since conception. What a remarkable experience! Tomorrow I will call my doctor for a complete confirmation of the good results that I received today.

⬅ SEPTEMBER 26, 1980

Tomorrow I enter my fourth month and today I saw my doctor for a checkup. I am approximately fourteen to fifteen weeks pregnant. He gave me a good report, having heard the fetal heart sounds today. He said I should be able to hear the baby's heart in another four weeks. I might even be able to "feel life" as well.

I still get waves of nausea in the morning, but not as often as before. The sickly feelings don't continue throughout the day any more. The spotting stopped about the second week of my third month—which means I can probably start exercising soon. I've gained only two pounds, but my pants are very tight. I bought more maternity clothes this week and yet I am afraid I am going into them way too early. I still fit into skirts and dresses, but pants are almost impossible to wear. I've noticed that if I diet—no cookies, cakes, breads, or potatoes—then I really feel less bloated and tired! I was watching my diet closely until about a week ago and then sure enough, I got the munchies and gained two pounds!

⬅ OCTOBER 17, 1980

Today I completed seventeen weeks of pregnancy. Next Friday I see the doctor and enter my fifth month. The big news is that I felt "Life." On October 1, I was reading in bed at night and thought I felt those first tiny bubbles of life that are so hard to distinguish from gas bubbles. I felt the same bubbles four days later. But it wasn't until this past Tuesday during a new exercise class that I felt "life" while lying on my back just before doing the proverbial pregnancy sit-ups! The baby was probably saying "What's happening here?" Again last night, while lying motionless in my bed, I felt repeated strong kicks from the baby. It was exciting to share the moment with the little being inside of me.

∽ JANUARY 7, 1981

I am almost half way through my seventh month. Time really seems to be flying by. I am still feeling pretty good but I am quitting exercise class because my back hurts and I feel kind of fat and clumsy. I am tired lately. For the first time I have cleaning help, which is so welcome because it is hard to keep up with the four-bedroom house and two kids. During the day Ali is in school and Tony spends time with me either playing or running errands. I have trouble sleeping, so I spend many nights on the couch in the den.

This baby also seems to kick a lot. The other night, I fell asleep at about ten o'clock. When my husband, Shawn, came home from a business trip, I got up to talk with him for a while. Then I tried to go back to sleep but the baby was moving so much I couldn't even lie down. It felt like the baby had the hiccups. Today while I was driving, the baby moved so much that it felt like these sharp little feet (or knees and elbows) were falling out of my stomach! Interestingly, when I don't eat very much, I can feel the baby more. I am convinced that when I lie down, I can identify body parts—a foot, a back or even a "tushy" poking out or moving around. Watching my belly is like a silent symphony of motion.

I no longer have strong feelings about the sex of this baby. I think that Alicia wants a sister, but I know that Tony wants a brother for sure. I was positive it was a girl until my doctor said "boy's heartbeat." I am not so sure he is right—but then again, I am not so sure that I am right either. Some days I feel more like I am carrying a boy because I look pregnant straight out in front just like when I carried Tony. But then I relate to other things like light weight gain and feelings that I had when I was pregnant with Alicia, and I think it's a girl.

I have just bought the first, new baby layette items: a snuggle bag, a baby journal, a picture frame, and the new Teddy Bear that quiets a crying baby with taped interuterine noises that sound like the ocean surf and beach waves rolling in to shore. I am sure I will have plenty of time to get the nursery ready because I always deliver late. With my due date at March 27, I could even spill over into April. I know I would be mentally ready for a delivery anytime after March 15. With my propensity for numerological analysis, I calculated the perfect date as March 11 because Tony was born on April 12 and Alicia on May 13. March, April, May—11, 12, and 13. Silly me and my need for perfection!

∽ FEBRUARY 2, 1981

It's 4 P.M. Tony is playing with his daddy, Ali is in the bathtub, and I am about to get dressed to go to a Chinese dinner party. I have been meaning to write in this diary for a while to report on my seventh-month doctor's checkup but I have been too busy and too tired.

During January I got a sinus flu that really got me down for one full week. It came on fast one morning, attacking me with fever, aches, stuffed head, and chills—all by nighttime. I was out of commission for several days, sleeping most of the time and eating very little. Alas, a little loss of weight! Time is the only healer and the hours and days seem to tick by sluggishly slow.

Time did settle the situation, and by January 20, when I saw my doctor for a regular checkup, I was back to normal. But the baby was transverse (sideways) again, instead of vertical with head down. Once again, signs point to a late delivery. I still have two months to get the baby in the right position (except for the fact that it is out of my control). A transverse delivery sounds scary.

∽ FEBRUARY 9, 1981

This sideways thing has really gotten to me. I keep worrying about delivery, especially with my due date only seven weeks away. The baby kicks side-to-side most of the time, and sometimes that really frustrates me and drains my emotions. It is a constant reminder that everything is not right nor ready yet. Last night, at about 1:30 A.M., I woke up with extreme discomfort. Something tells me that the baby turned and moved into position. The baby's kicks have been consistently high all day and I think that means it has turned around. I won't know for sure until February 20.

⌘ FEBRUARY 20, 1981

I am very relieved. The doctor tells me that this little baby has turned around and has nestled in with its head down and feet up. I will be seeing the doctor weekly now. Five weeks remain until my due date.

We have decided that Ali and Tony will move in together and share a bedroom when the baby arrives. Ali's room, the smaller of the two, is perfect for the nursery. I think the kids are beginning to get excited about the baby's arrival and about being roommates!

As for me, I finally feel fat! Hardly any space between boobs and hips isn't filled up with baby. To make matters worse, the doctor told me that the baby weighs only about four-and-a-half pounds. The baby is supposed to gain about a half-pound each week from now on, and eventually should weigh approximately seven pounds at birth. Once again, the doctor told me that he thinks the baby will be late. Oh well, we all must wait.

⌘ FEBRUARY 21, 1981

It is only two o'clock in the afternoon and yet this little baby has not quit moving and kicking all day. There have even been some super strong kicks just south of the boobs. I feel like my abdomen is filled up with 100 percent baby. I can't believe how many baby bumps and lumps I feel from just below my boobs, stretching all the way over to my left side, down and back up again. My lumpy bumpy body, the baby, and I will all be celebrating my twenty-ninth birthday tomorrow.

∽ MARCH 12, 1981

The ideal baby delivery date would have been yesterday—March 11. It would have coincided perfectly with three children born in March, April, and May on successive days. However, here I sit tonight, still very much pregnant—so much for perfect timing.

I have avoided writing in this diary for two weeks because I had some emotional and depressing experiences that have interfered with my excitement of getting ready for the baby's birth. I have a belly full of baby and a soul full of agony.

My personal state of bliss has been marred with problems. If I had tried to write in this journal, tears of devastation would have spilled onto each page. My spirits have been soaked in lonely isolation for I cannot share my sad emotions with anyone. Unexpectedly, I have had reason to question my marriage and suspicions have stabbed my heart and destroyed my confidence.

Even now as I write this, I feel helpless in my own ability to deal with the circumstances. For years now, my marriage has not been perfect and yet I have chosen to stay married and let motherhood be my center of attention and joy. My husband doesn't confide in me about all of his personal feelings and I feel very separate from his world. Sometimes I feel weak and dependent—emotionally and financially.

The birth of a baby is supposed to be a happy time—a blissful time to share lovingly with one's mate. However, I cringe in my isolation, for I know not the depths of my husband's mind. I am lost in traditionalism—love, honor, and obey. It appears that an emotional part of my husband lives in seclusion, away from me. I have my suspicions and am not sure if he has betrayed me, but it is clear that he is not sharing his whole self with me.

I tried to discuss my concerns with him, but he gave me no answers to my questions. So, nine months pregnant and feeling physically unattractive, I suffer alone. I ache with the daggers of depression that stab at my heart. I know what I must do: Close my eyes and pretend that nothing is wrong. I have to shed my doubts and feelings of insecurity. I must wrap my arms around myself for comfort. Hopefully, the new baby and motherhood will help me reclaim my sense of self in the darkness of this despair.

⤳ MARCH 15, 1981

To avoid dwelling on my sadness, I took Tony to the zoo yesterday. He delighted in the excursion and I was glad that I could pretend everything was fine. I am slowly trying to heal myself emotionally, but physically, I need to have this baby arrive soon. I bought new crib sheets, crib bumpers, quilts, and mattress covers in the past few weeks. I chose a tiny yellow rosebud pattern for everything, since I don't know if it is a boy or girl. All the baby bedding, clothes, blankets, etc. are washed and waiting. The infant seat and baby bathtub are scrubbed and ready. Today I picked up the baby announcements, that I helped design for a national card company based here in Minneapolis. I also packed my suitcase so I am ready, too, now that my due date is just two weeks away!

Actually, my pregnancy has gone by very quickly. I would probably have been more excited and overwhelmingly impatient by now if it hadn't been for my insecurities and fears. Unfortunately, I am the type who wants my life picture perfect and because I have been preoccupied with the unanswered questions in my marriage, I don't feel like I am mentally prepared for another baby.

Because I don't feel close to my husband, I am scared that I am emotionally unprepared for this addition to our family. The thought of another baby in this house, that we have already outgrown makes me fear that our family will be strained due to lack of physical space. I am also tired all of the time now and worry that I won't have enough energy for three kids.

My dear unborn child, I cannot put into words, without setting forth blame, the anguish and searing pain that has torn through my heart in the past few weeks. I dare not speak about that which I don't fully understand. I know that I should not disclose to you, precious child of innocence, the suspicions that prey on my mind.

In these past few weeks, I have reassessed my marriage and as reality has set in, I have become more disillusioned that things are not as "wonderful" as I had once dreamed they would be. I pray that the arrival of this third child will bring a rebirth to our marriage. At a minimum, perhaps we can settle back into a relaxed routine of easy living, arriving at a place where we can make the most of each day, appreciating what we have, without dwelling on what is missing in our daily lives.

I guess the ninth month of pregnancy is an emotional one at best, but when I add to that my desire to strive for perfect happiness, I place myself smack-dab in the middle of an ocean of impossibility. And that, dear baby, is where I have been drowning in my own thoughts and tears for the past few weeks.

⌒ MARCH 23, 1981

I am sitting here tonight, alone. A melancholy mood oozes from my pores. I am three days away from my due date and yet I am still emotionally unprepared for the birth of this baby. I have everything ready—suitcase, baby clothes, crib, and nursery—everything, that is, except me. I can hardly believe another baby will soon enter my life. I am uncomfortable now both day and night. I still recognize that a three-day waiting period can easily turn into a three-week marathon, especially with my history of being twice overdue. The thought of a new child in my life this weekend sounds overwhelming, and yet the thought of being pregnant for another twenty-one days sounds disastrous!

Last Friday I saw the doctor and the cervix was thinned out, but not dilated. He felt sure I would still be pregnant for another week. I am tired a great deal of the time now, and the baby's feet, with their wild random kicks, have made my skin feel as if it might tear from the pressured expansion. Last weekend I took a three-mile walk with my family around one of the city lakes. I was exhausted when we got home and for most of the week felt cramps coupled with contractions.

But now there is nothing. The doctor has forced me to put aside my earlier fears from when I was spotting and sick with the flu in my early months. I had been so afraid that something was going to be wrong with the baby. For a while my maternal intuition nagged at me and I nagged at my doctor. He ultimately faced me squarely: "There is nothing more that can be done to determine the health of this baby. We have performed all of the necessary tests already. You have to let go of your fears and take pleasure from the rest of your pregnancy. You will deal with whatever you need to when and if something happens." I took his stern lecture to heart.

MARCH 28, 1981

Here I sit in my tenth month of pregnancy! My due date was yesterday and I am officially overdue. All is well. I saw the doctor yesterday and the baby is in position, head down, with the cervix thinned out but closed. He feels that the baby is most likely a boy weighing between seven and seven-and-a-half pounds. As of yesterday, I have only gained twenty pounds but I feel like super blimp and fear that I will never be thin again.

I must be the most organized, well-planned domestic person. Before the birth of each baby, the laundry is always done, the house is spotless and in ready-to-go order with the kitchen cleaned two to three times each day. I constantly walk around putting things in their place while waging a mental war with myself asking "when?"

∽ MARCH 30, 1981

We haven't picked names at all yet. We have not even talked about it. But that is mostly because Shawn doesn't want to. I think about using the "J" name. It would be a religious tribute to his father, who passed away in 1979. My preferences today lean towards Jill, Joshua, or Justin. I would like to use the "E" middle initial to honor his father as well, which could mean Elizabeth or Evan. Perhaps, little one, you won't have a name for a while. But rest assured, we will do our best to give you one that you will love as much as we do you.

∽ APRIL 3, 1981

Jill Elizabeth Davis was born at 4:04 A.M., at Metropolitan Medical Center in Minneapolis, Minnesota. Weight: 9 pounds, 1 ounce. Height: 22 inches.

∽ APRIL 6, 1981

Metropolitan Medical Center

My dearest Jill:

I hadn't intended to write you a first "Message from Mommy" quite so soon, but the words just seem to be flowing. As you lie in your bassinet near me now, I can't help but feel love and pride that you are mine. It is early dawn; the morning sunrise is just moments away. There is a certain peacefulness that blankets my room as I watch you.

Strong overprotective feelings have developed in just three short days. I was on an "emotional hold" when you were born because of the pain. I actually saw you for the first time, upside down, with your long body stretched out—bottoms up! You were very, very red and screaming with your little face scrunched up. My first reaction was how swollen and dark you were. I was shocked that you didn't look like my child immediately, which makes no sense, since I'd never seen you before and I really didn't know what to expect.

You were born with a very dark complexion and a ton of thick black hair. Your eyes were swollen shut for the first fifteen hours of life. You cried from the moment of your birth through the first hour. When I went past the nursery window at eight o'clock in the morning, just hours after your birth, I saw that you were still screaming! Your face was so red and tensely scrunched and your small arms were shaking in an angry wailing cry.

Your birth was so different from my other children's. It was late evening on April 2, (just one week past your due date) and I was snuggled on the family room couch writing in Tony's childhood diary when I felt an extreme contraction at exactly 10:27 P.M. Something made me write down the time of that contraction as well as another one at 10:38 P.M. The bursting of "my water" immediately followed the two sharp pains, and I rushed to the bathroom in search of a towel to stop the flow onto the den couch and floor. Excitedly I yelled for your father, who had just gone to sleep. I also called my mother to come over and watch Ali and Tony.

We got to the hospital in a record twenty minutes. The contractions were not that strong, but they were coming every five to eight minutes. Nevertheless, the hospital staff readied me for your birth. The excitement of the quick progression of contractions and dilation kept me motivated through the next three hours. Labor progressed steadily with the contractions coming three minutes apart. Finally at 2:30 A.M. I got a shot for pain and by 3:00 A.M. when the doctor checked me, I was dilated to six centimeters. The nurse said that the baby's head was pressing right against the cervix and dropping nicely into position.

Soon the doctors and nurses were expressing glee that your head was "crowning." I kept insisting that your feet were jabbing into my upper ribs. The apparent incongruity of head and feet being so far apart made no sense until later when we learned of your long length. At eight centimeters dilation, I was wheeled into delivery where I started the hardest part of delivery.

I had been told that I was to have a caudal-type anesthetic, administered halfway through labor. Unfortunately, when I arrived at the hospital, I learned the only anesthetist who performed this procedure was on vacation. The immediate plan was to give me a local injection to block pain when the baby started to come, but that plan failed when your birth took on lightening speed at the end of delivery.

My only entertainment during those last thirty minutes of torture was the process of guessing baby gender and weight. The nurse predicted a girl based on the heart rate and she also guessed you would weigh about seven pounds four ounces. At the moment of birth, the nurse and doctor concluded that you would be closer to eight pounds. I remember the doctor commenting, "She has a lot of black hair." As I said, I saw you upside down for the first time, but I distinctly remember the total relief when you slipped completely out. I don't remember anything that I said, but I remember crying with exhaustion, relief, and elation when you were finally born. I remember wanting to name you Jill and I hoped your father would like the name.

I kept looking at you in total disbelief. I didn't think I had any preconceived notions, but for some reason, you didn't look like what I expected. My first visual impression was of a swollen, red, screaming baby and I was concerned at one point when you seemed blue in your delivery room bassinet. The doctors said you had been tightly "packed" inside me, hence the off-color.

Each day since your birth, your features have changed and your face has softly rounded out. Watching you sleep, even now, I can't believe how different you look in just a few days. I love to watch the movements of your dear little face. Your eyes, when they do open, are so expressive—looking around. You do such cute little things like scrunch up your petite mouth and make an adorable expression.

Since your birth, the long emotional hold of pregnancy has melted away. Even now, I am feeling very blessed that I have another daughter to love. I don't find myself comparing you to your sister; I seem to look at you individually. Despite all the pink flowers, bows, and presents, I still find it hard to believe that those days of pregnancy, days of feeling fat and uncomfortable, have produced a wonderful, live, healthy precious person after all. I can't believe that in just a few hours I will be taking a sweet little girl home to our house to be our new little daughter and sister.

Jill, you have made our family complete. Ali and Tony came to visit you at the hospital yesterday. They put on adult-sized hospital gowns to come into my room and peer into your hospital bassinet. They looked so grown up and proud as the big sister and brother! But you are so tiny in comparison to them!

I pray that I will be a good mother to you all. I want to love you and share life with you in a special way. I feel very blessed to have you. There is a lot of love waiting for you at home. My dear little Jill Elizabeth, please allow me to grow up with you. To grow and learn, particularly, how to be the best mother that you and your siblings deserve. I have learned a great deal about mature mothering since Ali was born and I now have high expectations for myself, especially since I have been blessed with two daughters and one special son. You, the last star to fall from the sky, have made my dreams and family complete.

⌒ APRIL 7, 1981

Dear Jill,

At 6 A.M., the nurse woke me to take my temperature. I slept all night.

It suddenly feels like "BOOM"; the "baby blues" have hit. I feel as though I am going to cry. In the past few days, despite my exuberance and elation, I have been worried about you. You have been spitting up all the time. I just went down to the nursery to see how you did last night—especially since you threw up so much of your feeding at 11:00 last night.

A really sweet nurse, who worked all night, knew I was worried. When she fed you during the night, she watched to see what might be the problem. She said I would have to watch you very carefully because you are a "gulper." She said you need to burp every half-ounce, and sometimes even more often. Since you gasp for air quite frequently, she suggested I stop the feeding whenever you need to slow down to avoid spitting up.

Today is our day to go home. Your first four days in the hospital have been filled with the normal new baby things of newborn gifts, flowers, and first impressions. On your first day of life, crying seemed to dominate your activities. You spent most of the time wriggling with your eyes closed and your brow wrinkled. At one point, I passed the nursery window and commented: "She looks so worried, as if she is going to have a nervous breakdown before she is one day old!"

By the second day, your color was better. You weight was down to eight pounds twelve ounces. Your eyes were still swollen but open and you seemed more alert. By evening you had taken six feedings, each averaging one-and-one-half ounces, although your evening feeding included a full two ounces! I kept you in my room and often I would just watch you sleep while I wrote in your diary or rested in my bed. Sometimes, I actually had to wake you to eat, which you did, even though you remained sleepy. Your dad brought Ali and Tony to visit you at the hospital and I took pictures of them standing tentatively next to your little hospital bassinette even though you slept through their visit.

Yesterday I called the rabbi to talk about your Hebrew name. In the Jewish religion, it is tradition to name a newborn for someone in the family who has passed away. Your grandfather, Julius, is the only deceased relative in your lineage. His death from cancer, just two years ago, was traumatic and sudden. To remember him by using the same initials or name would be a tradition and an honor.

I chose the name "Gila Aviva" which means Jill or Joy. The literal translation for Gila in Hebrew is "My joy is from the Lord." Aviva means Youthful Spring. Your name, Jill Elizabeth, Gila Aviva, makes me think of springtime joy.

Your grandmothers came to see you yesterday. You actually slept through their visit. I tried to wake you for a few feedings, and when I did manage to get you to eat at 10:30 A.M., you spit up again. The pattern is somewhat disconcerting. But despite my anxiety about your eating difficulties, I am excited (and nervous) about taking you home today.

Right now you are lying in your bassinet sleeping. It is still early morning—the peaceful time when silence allows meditation and reflection. I am watching you sleep. It is almost like I am looking, for the first time, at a beautiful little round face. When you were born, your head was molded due to the birth canal. Because your cheeks were so pudgy, the bottom of your face seemed wider than your forehead! To make matters worse, your dark hair stood straight up on end, an electrified disarray. You actually had such a foreign look with your deep coloring that we thought you were of Native American heritage.

But now, as I watch you sleep, you look peaceful and sweet. Your face is full and round when you are at rest and your complexion and facial expressions are dear. I have captured this extraordinary look on film. It is a picture of sweetness and serenity, and one that I will treasure for years to come.

☜ THURSDAY, APRIL 9, 1981

Dear Jill,

So far we have had two great days at home. Everyone has enjoyed your arrival. We have a port-o-crib set up in the dining room so that we can see and hear you at any time. Ali and Tony actually stand on the dining room chairs (or little stools) to look at you and watch you sleep. I forget that they haven't had very much time with you since you were born. Having you home is special.

You have been sleeping beautifully from feeding to feeding, although it takes about forty-five minutes per bottle. Burping you is still difficult because you cough and sputter, plus you seem to drink each bottle so slowly. Your chest feels raspy sometimes too.

Today you slept on your tummy more often. I still have to wake you for some feedings. Your only fussy period seems to be between five and six o'clock, which of course is our family dinner hour. You usually cry yourself to sleep while we eat our dinner and then of course, you have the Teddy Bear with the maternal womb sounds right there in your crib with you. The bear works like magic to help you fall asleep when you need it the most.

Generally, you have been eating five to six times per day (an average of two-and-a-half ounces), but unfortunately, you still spit up (or throw up for that matter) at least once or twice. When I left the hospital on Tuesday, I asked the pediatrician if the spitting up, raspy breathing and nasal congestion were all normal. He said that, in his opinion, your skin color was good and he did not think anything else was abnormal. Instead of really answering my questions, he commented on a patch of skin by your groin that might darken into a birthmark later. I was left wondering.

The big news yesterday was the fact that you found your thumb! Two times. You like to sleep on your side, sort of, although I generally place you in your crib on your stomach for each nap. You spontaneously smiled for the first time three days ago and it seems that you were quite happy these past two days.

I still get anxious and somewhat uncomfortable feeding you, however, because I am not sure what I am doing to cause you to spit up so often. I have always loved feeding babies and cradling them in my arms but for whatever reason, I am tensing up when I feed you. Yesterday I asked Ali and Tony to leave the room while I fed you your bottle thinking I needed the peace and quiet to coax you into a smooth feeding. It is hard on them to be "dismissed" but I am struggling to relax at feeding times with you.

I have also noticed a deepening of your skin color during bath time. I wondered if you were extremely chilled or if your ruddy complexion was natural and unique only to you. The grayish rust seemed so odd that I quickly wrapped you up in the warmth of your hooded baby towel to protect you from the cold.

I write down the amount of formula you drink at each feeding and I watch the naturalness of your sleep patterns between each feeding. I don't have much to compare to, but my analytical nature suggests that since you were a bigger baby than your brother, Tony, you should be eating more than he did at this age.

You are on what I would call a demand-feeding schedule. This allows you to sleep until it is time to eat again, or until you get hungry. Logic suggests that if babies generally wake whenever they get the urge to eat, then you, a bigger baby than most, should be waking more often—especially since you don't eat that much at each feeding. The opposite seems to be true. I actually have to wake you up for feedings. I am not sure of the significance of this pattern, but I am recording the details so I can watch your growth and progression. I may call your pediatrician, Dr. Blum, to check on your development.

☙ SUNDAY, APRIL 12, 1981

Dearest Jill:

Life works in very strange ways. I always envisioned that my life would not be complete without a third baby. When you were born, Jill, I assumed my family and marriage were now picture perfect. But from your birth, I have had a strange feeling whenever I would look at you and try to comprehend that you were undeniably my youngest daughter. I grew to love you very quickly. Despite the fact that you were a robust, nine-pound baby, I intrinsically knew that you were my sweet, fragile, little girl. Maternal instinct and feminine intuition sometimes have a pull so strong that the sensation is more frightening than it is profound.

On Friday I must have sensed something was not right with your schedule or system, and I anxiously called Dr. Blum, not once, but twice. My first call alerted him to my concern. As always, I detailed my analytical thinking for him—questioning the quantities you ate against the amount you slept between feedings. His advice was to watch you closely throughout the weekend, and if things did not improve by Monday to bring you in to his office. But it was my second call, at 4:30 P.M., to the pediatric nurse advisor, which produced results. After hearing my tense questioning and fearful confusion, she commented, "Mrs. Davis, you don't sound right. Why don't you bring the baby in to see the doctor immediately rather than waiting until Monday?" Jill, it turns out that those few words saved your life that weekend.

Racing off to the doctor at close of business on a Friday afternoon was not the easiest task to pull off under normal circumstances. Add the ingredients of two toddlers, a postpregnant worn-out woman trying to adjust to new motherhood, and a newborn to the mix, and you have what was a very tense situation.

Interestingly enough, I had called your father to come home and help me with the three children because I was bleeding badly and was exhausted from postpregnancy recovery. He arrived home just as I placed Ali and Tony in the bathtub and I departed for what I thought was going to be a reassuring and comforting visit to the pediatric doctor's office.

I will never forget the moment that they told me you were in heart failure and suffering from a severe congenital heart defect. It was not just one doctor but two senior members of the pediatric group who calmly gave me the terrifying news. There I stood in that tiny sterile examination room watching you lay helplessly "blue" and all alone on the papered table.

Our heritage comes back to haunt us at the most surprising moments. I remember thinking "Oh my God, is she going to have a scar?" It was a fleeting moment later that I shed my parents' paranoia about beautiful bodies and tearfully asked if you were going to die. The doctors said they didn't know.

Now, two days later, we still don't know too much else.

You are in the Life Support Unit (LSU) at Minneapolis Children's Hospital. We have great trust in your doctor and in your care. Tomorrow I will know more about your heart problems, your specialized care, and how they will make you better.

Just two nights ago, I thought you were going to die. I cried all night in fear of losing you, the last child I was given to love. Yesterday I found new hope. I believe that you will live and you will be my special baby to care for. Your defective heart, as bad as it is, is what makes you more precious to me. You represent a young life to hold on to, a life we must work hard to keep, and a special baby to love in appreciation of the gift of having you in our lives.

I hope you will live, Jill. You can be taken from me at any time—and my heart aches to bear that thought. We've been so blessed in our lifetime. My philosophy has always been that everyone is given something in life to bear as a hardship. I am suddenly convinced that you were given to me to make me stronger, to make me a better mother, and to help me grow into a mature woman. At twenty-nine years old, I have been sheltered and protected. Now it is my turn to shelter and protect you. Please, Jill, keep fighting. Stay in our lives. I want to love you and keep you safe.

᥌ TUESDAY, APRIL 14, 1981

My darling Jill,

These past four days have been filled with much emotion and information. On Friday, April 10, I called your dad to pick me up at the doctor's office and drive us to the Children's Hospital. I had volunteered there for one year, and interestingly enough, the one part of the hospital that scared me the most, the intensive care Life Support Unit, is the one where you are. We arrived at 5:30 and they ran tests until eight o'clock. I brought Ali and Tony upstairs to the "Child Life" Department. They played in a hospital playroom, preoccupied with dozens of toys and were cared for by the nurse friends I had cultivated throughout the year.

We met with your new doctor, Dr. Harold Katkov, a pediatric cardiology specialist, to learn of your diagnosis. At 8:30 we went home, physically and emotionally spent, and stunned by the events of the day. Scotch on the rocks and emotional phone calls to confused relatives consumed the rest of our evening until we fell into bed, hoping sleep would disintegrate our anxiety and pain.

Bright and early Saturday morning, I went back to the hospital to see you. What a difference! Your color was so much better. Your face was pink and beautiful. The swelling around your eyes had disappeared and your fingers and toes were no longer blue. Your eyes were open and your tiny fingers held my hand. You looked sweet, beautiful, and fragile.

The doctors had you on oxygen, along with digitalis and other intra-venous medicines. You were hooked up to ominous monitors. I was suddenly observing, quite visibly, your rapid heart rate of 160-170 beats per minute. Your rapid breathing was out of sync as well. Even your feeding was affected. You were tube-fed and you ingested only one-and-a-half ounces of formula. The medicines for your heart failure have affected your weight by pulling excess fluid from your body. That is why your color is better and the swelling is way down. But so is your weight. The robust, ruddy-colored infant, who weighed in at nine pounds at birth is now attached to tubes and monitors, lying in an intensive care bassinet, and weighing only seven and a half pounds.

∽ WEDNESDAY, APRIL 15, 1981

Good morning little Jill:

It is 6:30 A.M. You have become even more precious now as our delicate critically ill baby. You are still very, very sick, but we feel you are holding on to life with all your strength. I have felt three times since Friday night that my baby was going to be lost and taken from me. But now I have new hope that you will survive and be our miracle baby.

I have never seen your father so overwhelmed by a little baby as he is by you. Watching his vulnerability is remarkable, given the fact that he truly is the quintessential controlling authority figure—an impenetrable model of strength. He just comes to the hospital and looks at you, so fragile and delicate; I can see quite visibly his strong feelings. Painful expressions of a lack of control are written on his face as he helplessly watches you sleep. He tells everyone how beautiful you are, and he seems to care about you, your survival, and your life as if it were the most important thing in the world.

Since Friday night you have undergone extensive bedside testing and yesterday you had an important diagnostic procedure called a heart catheterization. You also had an emergency surgery on Sunday morning. The procedure, called a coarctation repair, was designed to open an artery that was almost completely closed. It was a major artery that prevented free-flowing blood to your lower extremities.

The doctors described the severity of this particular procedure. When it was first introduced at the University of Minnesota several years ago, more than 50 percent of the infant patients died during surgery. Your odds did not seem much better in 1981. But you survived and the surgery was considered a success. As a result, blood flow was increased to all parts of your body.

In intensive care you have survived two dangerous procedures. You are still critically ill, under constant watch, hooked up to countless tubes, enduring a myriad of tests and medications. Your life is still in delicate balance. You are not cured, but you remain stable and the doctors can move forward to try and let you sustain your life on your own. They will begin by letting you breathe and function on your own, hopefully ingesting food and maintaining a healthy balance. You could still be critical for another ten days. You may even need more surgery.

They have explained everything to us over and over again. You have three serious heart defects—only one of which was corrected by Sunday's surgery. The other two anomalies need further surgery, but hopefully they will wait until you are older, bigger and better able to stand the strenuous procedure.

Your defect is actually called "Transposition of the Great Vessels, double outlet with a ventricle septal defect." No child has ever survived your birth defect. If you survive, you will be a precious, fragile baby girl with a long road ahead of you. Two more surgeries, medications, and specialized care are part of your future. You are likely to be a small child until you are older and stronger. There is hope that you can one day be a normal healthy girl who can run and play like other children.

There is so much to think about now. I want to tell you how much we love you and how much you mean to us. You are so special and I am convinced that you have been given to us for a reason. I believe that our love will have to pull you through and help you survive life as a heart baby. I wonder if your birth wasn't meant to pull your dad and me closer together, and to help me mature and be a stronger woman. I wonder if your birth wasn't meant to teach me how to cope with life's REAL problems.

I wanted to hold you so desperately yesterday, Jill. Momentarily, I had real faith that you may be coming home again. Every time I see you I know I feel love and a special caring for you. But more than that, I yearn to help you. Your nurses and doctors are working their medical miracles. With my love added to their expertise, I am convinced we have the magic formula.

∽ WEDNESDAY, APRIL 22, 1981

Dear Jill,

I have been so afraid to write down my feelings since last Wednesday when you had yet another emergency surgery. On that day, I was so afraid that each time I wrote down my hopeful feelings there would be another disastrous setback. They tell me you are stable once again and progressing, even though we have periods of backward movement.

The days have been filled with turbulent emotion. I get confused sometimes about what happened when. On Sunday you had the surgery to repair your narrowed aorta. Monday, you were stable. Tuesday, you had a serious, unstable morning; but you managed through a heart catheterization in the afternoon. On Wednesday April 15, you had a critical morning with a bad turn toward heart failure. The doctors felt your only chance was to go into surgery one more time for a procedure called "pulmonary banding." This was clearly a lifesaving procedure because the blood was flooding your lungs. Amazingly, you once again survived surgery. The gushing of enormous amounts of blood to your lungs ceased and you seemed to be doing a little better. As before, I was afraid to get too excited about your progress even though the doctors were pleased with your postoperative condition.

Thursday, you were stable and slowly waking up from your heart surgery. Friday through Sunday, your progress was steady and I finally allowed myself to think days ahead. I even began to think about you coming home. Late Sunday, however, it became obvious that you were having some difficulty keeping more than two ounces of formula down and you threw up several times both Sunday and Monday.

Yesterday, you lost three feedings in a row. Today, my fear and concern have increased. Even your dad shares my tension. The doctors have finally decided to test you for several possible causes of the repeated vomiting.

Your digestive condition has been only one tension in the past few days. We have experienced multiple moments of trauma including a collapsed lung, heart failure, and cardiac arrests. During extremely dangerous situations, the doctors flooded your veins with lifesaving medications to bring back your stilled heart. Unfortunately, your little left hand was severely burned when you had a cardiac arrest and the doctors had to administer the drug Calcium intravenously, to save your life. Unfortunately, the powerful drug burned your arm as it was injected into your body through a vein that rested terribly close to the skin's surface. With the instability of your heart, the doctors had no choice but to push the drug through the vein that possessed the greatest potential for saving your life, despite the inherent risks.

I was home on complete bed rest when all of that happened. My doctor had threatened to put me in an adult hospital if my postpartum bleeding didn't limit itself to a normal level. The fact that you were nine pounds at birth, coupled with the fact that I lost another nine pounds in labor and delivery meant that I quickly dropped eighteen of the twenty pounds gained in pregnancy. The rapid weight loss was only significant in that it demonstrated my body's vulnerability to further trauma. The stress of your hospitalization contributed to my weakness and the doctors hoped that bed rest would stop the excessive bleeding.

By the time I returned to Children's Hospital, although I was still weak, I was eager to see you again. I was also conditioned to view your burn sites as a grateful gift. I now believed that the medicine that had caused them had also saved your life. I was quickly developing a reinforcing dichotomous approach to the "body beautiful" concept that my parents preached. I was learning to be appreciative of the body disfigurements that validated your warrior and survivorlike capabilities.

Your extensive medical testing during the past few days also included a barium x-ray to determine if your stomach was obstructed or malformed. The results showed no problems whatsoever. You were also tested for infections through urine samples, blood samples, and nasal/throat cultures. Your infant formula was changed with no immediate results, so the diagnosis is still unresolved. The only good news, it seems, is that certain serious ailments have been ruled out as diagnostic possibilities. Thank God.

As of 1:30 P.M. today you were put on intravenous feedings and your regular bottles have been discontinued for twenty-four hours while we wait for further answers. While today wasn't easy, yesterday was the heartbreaker. I helped give you a bath. I nearly cried when I saw how terribly thin you are. You still weigh only seven-and-a-half pounds and your arms and legs look just pathetic! I fear you will never gain back the weight. I want to scream or cry and then hold you and squeeze you to make you all better. But I know I can't.

I also hate going home from the hospital because that means I am away from you. I miss you. I really can't think of anything but you. Sometimes I feel it is unfair for Ali and Tony to have me gone so much of the time. They don't really understand what is going on. All they know is "Jill is very sick." Tony had his birthday last week and we couldn't even have a party due to your hospitalization. The grandmas were wonderful as they filled in the gap of missing parents.

At the hospital, I can block out everything that doesn't relate to you. When I hold you, your eyes stare piercingly at me, with what appears to be a helpless pleading asking me to assure you that everything will be okay. Oh, how I wish you would just get well. I am running out of strength, but you never seem to give up. That demands that I never quit trying as well. Keep up the fight, little one. You are a fighter. I believe in you.

∽ MONDAY, APRIL 27, 1981

Dear Jill,

Today you moved from the Life Support Unit to the fourth floor (4 West) of Minneapolis Children's Hospital. Progress. Life has certainly changed perspective. We now measure your weight in kilograms instead of pounds and your intake of fluids in cubic centimeters instead of ounces.

I even slept here at the hospital with you in a makeshift chair bed. You were restless as I watched you sleep. You cried from the ten o'clock feeding until midnight. You only quieted down when I held you and walked with you in my arms.

In the past few days, I have meticulously watched every detail of your medical care—vital statistics through electronic monitors coupled with multiple conversations with your attending physicians and nurses. I thirst for information and answers.

You have survived emergency surgeries, heart failure and arrests, a collapsed lung, respirators, and heart catheterizations. You have had serious episodes of arrhythmia and tachycardia—unstable and fast heart rhythms. When you slipped into heart failure, emergency measures with their serious side effects were successfully employed. Each time you had a heart operation, you slowly woke up from the anesthesia and the effects of curare, a drug administered to immobilize the body during heart procedures. Your cardiologist told me that there aren't more than ten babies in the world who have survived what you have gone through so far. One of your surgeries, the coarctation repair, when first used, had an average survival rate of one of every two babies across the United States.

A week ago Saturday, I held you in my arms for the first time since you have been hospitalized, IV tubes and all. You have graduated from umbilical cord feedings to half-strength baby formula administered through a baby bottle. Unfortunately, you continue to spit up what I consider massive amounts after each feeding.

Your weight is now about 3.6 kilograms. Actually, it fluctuates from 3.43 to 3.65. Your heart rate is usually about 140 beats per minute and your respiration 60–68. Some of your feedings have been as high as 75 cc. And actually you once took a full 80 cc of formula. I have learned to correlate the number of ccs of formula with each pound of weight gain so that I can monitor your growth. I get excited when I see you ingest more than 60 cc (or two ounces) of formula. However, you continue to lose whole feedings with your vomiting.

Five days ago they began additional medical testing in search of a diagnosis for the vomiting and disruptive feedings. You had blood tests and a barium x-ray to confirm pyloric stenosis. The test came back negative. For the past four days you have been on antibiotics. You have also started crying after each feeding. We are questioning why. You are on half-strength baby formula. When they switched formula to something called Pregestim, you hated it even more. We are still perplexed as to the best solution for your eating problems.

∽ APRIL 30, 1981

Dear Jill,

Today your doctor requested an additional x-ray to diagnose the reason for your perpetual vomiting. We finally got an answer! Gastroesophageal reflux—grade 2+. What that means, is the muscle that closes off the stomach after eating is underdeveloped and therefore it causes formula to rise back up again after it has been ingested. We can solve the problem by mixing rice cereal with the formula (to weigh it down). We can also feed you differently to keep your body tilted upright during and after each feeding. We are hopeful that that should help.

∽ MAY 2, 1981

Dear Jill,

This was your last full day in the hospital. You had eight feedings, each one averaging 65–70 cc. You only "lost" the 9:30 P.M. feeding, but you managed to keep another 60 cc at 10:30 P.M. You get to go home tomorrow.

∽ SUNDAY, MAY 3, 1981

Age: One month old. Home from the hospital!

∽ THURSDAY, MAY 8, 1981

Dear Jill,

Well, my little lady, you were home all of three days and now you are back in the Life Support Unit at Children's. Sunday, your homecoming day, was really pretty nice. You slept well, some feedings stayed down, and only once did I worry about you.

For just one moment, you looked like you had trouble breathing while you were vomiting and I thought you might have aspirated while throwing up. While you were eating, you kept crying and arching your back in apparent agony. I had a long discussion with a pediatrician on Monday and we decided that it was not your formula that was causing the discomfort. Instead, we deduced that it must be due to a good case of constipation! So we switched you to one teaspoon of prune juice in a bottle, one time per day to solve the problem.

On Monday evening, I had to rebandage your burned hand. The burn, still quite severe, requires dressing changes daily. Last

Monday, when I had the responsibility for cleansing the wound, it seemed extra swollen. At 8:30 P.M., I met a doctor at the Children's emergency room to see if anything was wrong. Routinely, they took your temperature, only to discover it was elevated to 100.4°. We questioned whether your arm was infected.

On Tuesday, I saw your regular physician, Dr. Blum, and again your fever was up. So was your white blood count. A reading of 22,000 definitely meant an infection of some sort. He started you on oral antibiotics. The good news was that your weight was up to 8 pounds 2 ounces. For twenty-four hours I was pleased with your progress. You kept all your formula down for most of that day.

By Wednesday afternoon you became more lethargic and your feedings dipped to only one or two ounces every few hours. I took you back down to the Emergency Room and you were re-admitted to Children's with a fever of 101.4°.

When you were readmitted your weight was 3.82 kilograms (8 pounds 6 ounces) They treated you with IV antibiotics and warm saline packs to your left arm to bring down the swelling. Your arm was burned, swollen, and lumpy almost up to the shoulder. Your tiny fingers were puffy and red. Your arm stayed limp by your side. You clearly favored the inactivity and I assumed you were in great pain. You cried intensely whenever anyone touched it. By Thursday (May 7), you required additional surgery to drain the infected fluids from your arm.

The procedure was called incision and drainage (I and D). The surgery really had two purposes: one, to drain out the infection, and the other, to biopsy the lumpy tissue to determine the type of infection. A pediatric surgeon did the surgery, bringing the total number of medical specialists attending you to four (pediatrician, pediatric cardiologist, thoracic surgeon, and now pediatric surgeon). They were all the "best of the best" and our confidence level sustained our high hopes each time you went under the knife and out of our control.

The fact that you had to go under general anesthesia for the I and D was of some concern to us all. Your heart condition remained delicate and dangerous and we weren't sure you could withstand the drugs used to put you to sleep for surgery. But when you came out of surgery okay, we waited impatiently, desperate to see if you would move your wounded arm after some of the swelling and pain diminished.

Finally on Friday we saw movement! Your alert behavior and delicate wriggling of those tiny fingers was a delight.

⌒ MONDAY, MAY 11, 1981

Dear precious little lady:

I am sitting here by your bedside in Children's Hospital. You have just fallen asleep—finally. You managed to keep down three ounces of formula, and yet you had another rough two days. Yesterday was Mother's Day. In the morning Ali and Tony tried to make the day special for me with breakfast in bed and little treats. It was a tough day, knowing that my children were not all together and one of them was lying in a hospital bed alone.

During the morning, you vomited the majority of your feedings. I came to visit you just after noon, and you did manage to keep down 80 cc of formula for me. Your skin color is "yucky" but your eyes are bright today.

In the afternoon, your grandmas went over to our house to be with Ali and Tony so that your dad could visit you too. You smiled three times for him. The doctors tell us your arm is getting better although I was terribly upset to learn that your skin most likely will be permanently scarred due to the depth of the burn on your arm. I don't think I ever really grasped the severity of the burn. You may even need skin grafts or plastic surgery, depending on how you heal.

You and I seem so separate again. The closeness we shared when you were home for those three short days seems lost. I don't feel that you really know me like you did last week. My heart aches to think of you so lonely and insecure here in the hospital by yourself. And I feel so helpless when I leave you each night to go home. I hate to think that any of your babyhood is slipping away without the normal physical touching, cuddling, and loving. I still can't pick you up and hold you like a normal baby. I miss you and want you home, but I want you well.

I still can't bear to think of what the future holds for us. There is a possibility that you might not survive your corrective surgery later this year. It is a difficult procedure, but we have hope that you will do okay. The fact that no child has ever survived your open-heart procedure does not change our faith in your perseverance.

Yesterday I felt dejected that I had to visit you, my baby, in a hospital, on Mother's Day. But then I couldn't bear to think that next year you might not even be here. You are sleeping now. Rest well, little sweetheart, and get better for me. Do a good job for us. I love you so.

ᖗ MAY 14, 1981

Dear Jill,

I am sitting by your isolation room watching you sleep. Rest up, little baby, for you have a busy day ahead of you. Your arm wound has healed sufficiently to allow you to go home today, almost for sure. But before you are discharged, you will be seeing a physical therapist for instruction on how to exercise your left arm and fingers.

You have had little spontaneous movement in your arm or hand since the chemical burn. The swelling and pain of the burn must have also contributed to what appeared to be a semiparalysis. This morning a pediatric surgeon is planning to "clean up" the burn site a bit more, and he will also teach me how to care for the wound and change the bandage. You are also going to be visited by a cardiologist for another checkup. We will probably get a long list of instructions before going home. Thank goodness your reflux problem has settled down during the last two days. You have been alert, smiling and resting well enough to be sent home.

MAY 15, 1981

Jill, you are home from the hospital. Age: 6 weeks. Weight 8 pounds 3 ounces.

MAY 20, 1981

Dear Jill,

Today marks five full days that you have been home from the hospital. All my energy, both waking and sleeping, is devoted to keeping you strong and helping you. Your dad has been wonderful, helping with Ali and Tony, grocery shopping, and doing chores around the house. Ali is in school all day and Tony now goes to daycare part-time to make it easier for me. They seem to understand that my primary job is taking care of you, but I try and give them attention and hugs whenever I can.

I feel like I am fighting right along with you, to make sure that you lead a full life. I have never worked toward a more important goal than trying to get you through your upcoming heart surgery. A goal has never had so much purpose or been so vital. But what a nightmare, full of pain, lies ahead for us. For now though, I work each day through just giving you all your medicines, the therapy for your burned arm, bottle after bottle, and all the love I can. Bless you, little baby, for fighting for your own life. You must be a strong-willed warrior with an intense desire to live. You are so beautiful and wonderfully independent at such a tender age. You are very precious and dear to me.

∽ MAY 31, 1981

Good morning, Jill,

It is Sunday morning and you are still sleeping from your morning feeding of a half-jar of applesauce and six ounces of formula (you lost about one ounce when you threw up). This week has been a bit easier for us all because you are now sleeping through the night. Thank God for that!

Your arm continues to improve; the infection appears to be all gone. The burn wound is getting more red spots in it, meaning that more live, healthy tissue is appearing. The large hard calcium deposits seem to have softened a little but they are still there. Your fingers look normal much of the time, except for your middle finger (which still has a large hard bump in it)—it can't bend from the second knuckle back. All of the fingers are still a bit swollen but the color is better. You can move the whole arm all over, swinging it around, and sometimes you actually bump it and then start to cry.

The biggest hardship is still the feedings. Last Friday I got so frustrated that I yelled, slammed doors, got mad at you, and just cried from the sheer frustration of watching you vomit and lose your feedings. I don't know why it surprises me when you lose a feeding. Some days you vomit as much as six times. I should be used to it by now.

∽ FIRST WEEK OF JUNE 1981

Little Jill,

Your days are filled with feedings, vomiting up two or more feedings, medicines, physical therapy and doctors visits. You saw your pediatrician on June 3; the cardiologist and the pediatric surgeon on June 4. Your weight was 9 pounds 2 ½ ounces.

The reflux problem is still quite prevalent. You had some days when you seemed to be cramping and you screamed excessively.

We ultimately decided that your medicine made you crabby and we discontinued the reflux medicine. Much to our relief, you started to smile again!

Your sleep patterns are strange during the day, but you sleep great at night. You take catnaps during the day, maybe about forty-five minutes long after each bottle. Mornings are your toughest time. You generally throw up three times during the morning bottle. There are about six feedings per day, each averaging about five ounces. I give you your heart medicine, Lanoxin, morning and night and I do your hand/arm therapy three times per day—much to your dismay. When I place you on the kitchen counter, lying you down to clean the wound under warm running water, you shriek loudly with cries that pierce right through my heart.

I am not sure what your true personality is because I think you are in a great deal of pain much of the time. You have only been home from the hospital three weeks. Daily routine is so intense and the activities are so defined that the days drift into each other, highlighted only by how many ounces you eat or how stable your digestive processes are. There is a roller-coaster feeling to the passing of time.

Most of the time Ali and Tony stay away from me when I am taking care of you. I don't think they like your painful screams and I am sure they can sense my concern when I try to feed you or do your hand therapy. I am glad it is summer and they can be outside in the back yard playing together, away from my anxiety when I am taking caring of you.

Not often, but sometimes, they play near you, and I love to see Ali sitting quietly by your automatic swing, talking to you. The other day, Tony, wearing his blue Spiderman T-shirt, stood with you while you were swinging. He was busy chatting as you swayed back and forth. I am not sure who enjoyed the session more—you both had smiles on your faces.

Ever since you came home from the hospital, Ali and Tony have had to share a bedroom, which gives them added time together. They read books, play on their beds, or quietly talk (and giggle) when they are supposed to be asleep. I am glad they have each other. I think it is comforting for them to be in the same room, given all of the difficulties you are experiencing. I know they care about you and want you to be well, but I know they are also afraid.

ᨶ JUNE 14, 1981

Dear Jill,

Here I sit, exhausted after another long, emotional, tiring week. The week hit its high point when you weighed 9 pounds 10 ounces, which was a half-pound weight gain in just one week. The low point was this weekend when the doctors confirmed that your arm infection had returned. You were in great pain, with a fever of 100–101°.

It is so depressing to have one week up and one down, especially when our goal is make progress toward enough weight gain so that you can withstand the open-heart surgery needed to repair your defective heart. My heart aches to look at your precious face during a peaceful moment when you are sleeping. It is in those tender moments that I can't begin to comprehend all that you have been through.

When I look for a smile or a special twinkle in your eye, I cry at the thought that you have never really been yourself. Between heart surgeries, cardiac arrests, medical treatments, and trauma, you have been in pain or discomfort much of the time. You have had stomach pain and cramping and pain from your burned arm. Add to that the fact that I have to manipulate your burned arm three times each day, scraping out calcium deposits to encourage healing. That alone causes you additional, excruciating pain. I often ask myself: "When will this precious little one be free of pain and be happy in a joyful, playful normal manner?"

Sometimes I hate myself in the midst of caring for you. I selfishly get angry with you because you scream or fuss or vomit yet another traumatic feeding. So often I forget how much you must be suffering and I am only reacting to evidence of that pain. How much pain do you really feel? Oh, how I wish I could make you all better.

When you smile, I melt. Why can't you be happy and smile more often? Why can't you be more like normal babies? Oh, how my heart aches because I can't make you better. I squeeze you with love and kiss you over and over again. But it never helps. Please go away, pain. Let the sunshine bring a smile to my baby.

∽ JUNE 24, 1981

Dearest Jill,

It has been six weeks since you have come home from the hospital. Today we visited the pediatrician again. Now he suspects that you have colic because you cry so hard and cramp up so much. We started you on a new medicine, Levsin—PB, which is actually phenobarbital, an antispasmodic with a sedative. The new medicine calmed you down but as usual, you threw up—including the new drug. You also got very flushed after taking the medicine.

Jill, your arm is almost completely debrieded—only hard calcium deposits lay around the edges and somewhat in the middle. I feel like I sound so clinical in my description of your wound, but it truly is hideous to look at. Baby flesh is typically warm and soft, supple and pink. This burn is, by comparison, a huge open sore, with hard bits of calcium forming amidst the center of the sore. I learned that when the body has a severe burn, excess calcium forms at the site of the wound. The doctor suggested that I use a surgical tweezers to scrape the calcium out. I do that three times a day while you shriek with pain. We seem to be getting closer to healing, but we still must wait to see if your arm needs skin grafts.

The sore hasn't closed up yet, but it has filled in with healthy tissue. You still scream the minute I go toward your arm to remove the bandages for our daily therapy sessions. You know what's coming. Your fingers are still slightly swollen; the middle one is the worst. But your fingers actually curl more often now, and your upper arm seems to move normally. There is, however, little or no wrist movement.

Jill, you smile, but not often. You are most talkative late at night, although lately, for whatever reason, you haven't cooed at all during the day. Mornings are the time when you are the hungriest. You will you take more than eight ounces, even though you lose one to two ounces by vomiting. By evening, you get sleepy, full of cramps, and then you get cranky.

⌒ JUNE 27, 1981

My darling Jill:

You are sleeping soundly right now in the little crib in the corner of our dining room. You look so sweet and exquisitely petite. An aura of precious vulnerability encircles you as you lie there delicately breathing and passively resting your traumatized, malformed little body. I can't help but love you and cry inside because of all you must go through. Sure, I often feel sorry for myself because of the endless days of trouble in caring for you; but then I stop to think about who it is that really suffers.

I wish this were a nightmare and that you are not really hurting or in danger of dying. I wish that one day I will wake up to find a beautiful, sweet, healthy baby girl who has no scars, no pain, no screams, no breathing difficulties, and no horrible deformities of the heart. Each day I look at you, heartsick, because I know that I can't make it all go away. And that is when I am grateful for the little things—grateful that you are still beautiful and alive. I well up inside with appreciation for your mental alertness, your loving existence, and for my mere presence in your life.

I have so much trouble believing that I could ever lose you. Even though I complain that my life has dramatically changed, I really don't feel sorry for myself. You are the one with medical problems and life difficulties. I wanted a third baby so much and I know that all these long days of trouble will get better somehow, sometime in the future.

Today, as with so many mornings, you violently threw up and for a brief terrifying moment, you couldn't breathe. The baby formula got stuck in your nose and airway, causing you to suddenly panic as you stiffened your little body, waving your arms in response to your pain. Your eyes opened so wide and I panicked, screaming for your dad. By the time he came to help us, you were breathing and crying on your own. It was just another momentary melodrama, sandwiched in between the normal daily hardships and heartaches.

You have also been coughing for the past two to three days. I don't know why. I have been trying to analyze when and why you cramp up. Yesterday the intense screaming started at about 4:30 P.M. and lasted until 9 P.M. The most excruciating and painful screaming time comes between 8 and 9 P.M., but lately, the afternoon has rivaled evening for first place in screaming capabilities. I have noticed that holding you helps sometimes and walking with you in my arms seems to sedate you.

Speaking of sedation, I just did the opposite—I woke you up for your hand therapy and Lanoxin heart medicine. Then we will move right on to bath time and my favorite time—comforting and snuggling with you in my arms.

☜ JULY 7, 1981

Jill,

It has taken me four days to write this entry. You were three months old on July 3rd and a lot has happened in the last four days to make this entry quite different from the one I would have written last Friday.

A week ago I would have written about the pain, heartache, and frustration of taking care of you. There were days when I cried right along with you—hating the job of motherhood and the job of caring for a baby who continually cries and suffers so. I wanted desperately to get out of the tunnel in which I felt trapped.

Each day was the same and I dreaded waking each morning because it meant more of the same. Each day I felt emotionally compressed by the long hours of feeding you, manipulating your wounded arm in excruciating therapy, struggling to quiet you down while you cried and twisted in my arms for an hour at a time. I felt like I was breaking down mentally. The mixed-up feelings tortured me when I stopped to recognize that *you* were the one who suffered more than anyone.

Somewhere during the past few days I decided I just couldn't do it anymore. I couldn't continue poking at your tortured arm, wrestling with you, causing you additional pain and then fighting to calm you down. I also felt I couldn't keep up the intensity of counting every ounce of baby formula that you swallowed and kept down. I tried too hard and it hurt too much when you ate too few ounces. By keeping track of every ounce of liquid nourishment you ingested, I only hurt myself by knowing the pitiful amount you consumed.

So yesterday, I quit writing everything down. I asked the doctors if we couldn't discontinue arm therapy for one week, since I wanted to let your tender body rest just this once. They agreed! I still have to bathe your hand and arm three times a day in Dreft detergent to cleanse the wound, and I have to change the dressing to keep it clean. But I don't have to scrub it or scrape at it or poke around inside with the surgical tweezers at least for the next few days! What a relief!

I have also changed how I feed you. I let you eat as often as you like. Hopefully you will get on some sort of a reasonable schedule, like every three or four hours. I will do my best to offer you food whenever you are awake. So far, in just one day, the improvement has been dramatic! You talk all the time now! You started yesterday—talking in your infant seat for one hour while I worked near you in the kitchen. Then you talked the whole time we were at the doctor's office and last night you chatted to yourself all evening.

Again today you have been a little chatterbox. I gave you a bath and washed your arm and hair and yes, you cried, like always, but you immediately stopped when I picked you up and comforted you. What a joy! Now you are sleeping in your infant seat on the porch while I write in this diary. I feel as though we've entered a whole new world with you. Last night you giggled out loud while I played with you. Ali and Tony loved it! The mood has lifted. It is far more joyful. Just the other day, your grandmother danced with you in her arms and you chuckled out loud for her too. Mind you, your crazy mom was plenty upset that I didn't get to be the one to experience your first laugh.

As I look back on your first three months of life, I hope that I am closing an important chapter and turning the page to easier times. It's possible that you had three-month colic and that only time was needed to settle down the difficulties in eating and digestion. Whatever the reason, here's hoping things keep getting easier and the days ahead stay bright and beautiful for you, my little love.

⌒ JULY 12, 1981

Dear Jill,

You saw the pediatrician on Friday and weighed in at 10 pounds 9 ounces. I measured your length at home as 24 inches, but I don't know how accurate that is. Your days are filled with laughter and chatter now. You played with Ali and Tony today and when I held you up to the mirror, you talked to the baby image you saw. Your hand looks improved. I changed the bandage twice a day and the wound looks smaller, but you still cry when I wash it. Your middle finger is still quite big and hard and it curls in a strange way. You use the arm more normally most of the time, and there is a definite difference in strength.

You are waking up early and it still takes about an hour to feed you the morning bottle. Unfortunately, you still vomit several times a day. At the most, you only drink about eight ounces with each bottle. Your mornings are filled with hand therapy, after which you get another bottle, bath time, and baby catnaps in your infant seat where you love to sit and chatter to yourself.

Your third bottle is usually at noon or so and another follows in late afternoon when I give you your phenobarbital and repeat your hand therapy again. Sometimes while I am making dinner you sit in your infant seat on the living room floor while Ali or Tony play with you and keep you occupied. They love to hear you giggle and now that you are better, it is more fun for them to entertain you. After dinner, you usually sleep or play in your infant swing until I give you your last bottle of the day.

⌒ JULY 18, 1981

Dear Jill,

You are sleeping in your infant seat in the port-a-crib right now, looking so precious! You woke up, ate seven ounces of formula, and threw up two to three times before you ate again for another hour. You let me wash your arm a little; took your Lanoxin, and then fell asleep just sitting in your seat on the kitchen counter.

Your week has been pretty good. On Monday, we saw Dr. Roback, the surgeon, who measured your arm wound and discovered it is definitely smaller. The exciting discovery at your last medical visit was the fact that the top part of the open wound has closed up! It has also gotten shorter in length as well. We are talking fractions of centimeters, but to me it is a major breakthrough.

Your index finger and middle finger, however, still don't bend correctly. Both seem puffy and lumpy although you use the whole hand as if nothing is wrong. I can play hand games with you without you crying, now, and I can even pull you up with both arms, although there is a difference of strength.

The biggest concern I have right now is the total lack of wrist movement. The wrist feels hard and permanently straight; the hard calcium deposit is inflexible and unyielding. The immutable position scares me. The doctor tells me the wound might close up naturally and once that happens, we will have more physical therapy. Total healing time is estimated to be more than one year.

On the bright side of things: You have become a joyful baby to love and spend time with. I could play with you for hours and I do! I am with you constantly from 7 A.M. in the morning until 11 P.M. I even sleep on the floor of your room until you have rested long enough in your infant seat to digest your food. Once I have placed you gently in your crib, I return to my bed in my own room.

One night last week, while I slept exhaustedly on your floor next to you, your little body tumbled out of your infant seat right onto the floor! You were strapped in but somehow baby, infant seat and all, toppled over without waking you up. In the last few days you have increased your playfulness and smiling and your daily intake of formula. You watched television and joyfully played with Ali and Tony. You actually laughed out loud on Thursday, which was real music to my ears.

Last night, I cried inside because of the fear you are not going to survive your heart surgery next fall or winter. Yet I cannot believe you wouldn't make it. It is really unthinkable that I could lose you now.

If I am wrong, that my strong little daughter, who has fought the fiercest fight, does not survive her final heart operation, then I resign myself to the thought that I should not live either. I think, dear Jill, that if you don't survive then I will die inside too. I would feel so punished if I were to lose you. You are my whole life right now. Most of the time, you seem more important than anything else—which seems unfair because I have put my love for Ali and Tony on hold.

The hardest part of having you, Jill, is trying to understand my inner feelings. Why were you born to me with heart problems? I feel as though I must grow up. I feel I must suffer and learn in order to become a stronger person. But, God, how sorry I am that a precious, gorgeous child must suffer the emotional and physical scars and pain for *my* lesson in life.

Bless you, little one, for carrying this burden with me. God must have meant for me to suffer and I am sorry that you must too. I pray you will live and become a stronger, better, and more beautiful person than I could ever be. I love you, Jill.

☞ JULY 29, 1981

Dear Jill,

Tomorrow we have an appointment to see Dr. Richard Owens at Sister Kenney Institute of Abbott Northwestern Hospital. He is a doctor of physical therapy and hopefully, we can restore movement in your arm or at best prevent further damage.

My tenth wedding anniversary is just two days away. One year ago I began this journal of pregnancy and what has become a chronicle of life. My marital problems from a year ago seem to have temporarily faded, and you, my darling Jill, have taken the limelight and become the primary focus of our relationship. I don't know that we have repaired the flaws in our relationship, nor have we become closer, but we have learned to concentrate on that which is important and our old emotional baggage has drifted far from our daily thoughts.

You are doing wonderfully. You are happy, and you smile and laugh out loud regularly now. Jill, you respond to each of us—

your dad, mom, brother, and sister. You sleep all night, drink almost twenty ounces of formula a day, and your weight has reached 10 pounds 13 ½ ounces. You are 24 ⅝ inches long. And you still remain about the most important part of my life.

✍ AUGUST 3, 1981

Darling Jill,

You are four months old today. This is a very busy time for you. Jill, you are changing, doing more things, seeing more doctors, growing, and becoming more precious each day. Today you see the cardiologist, Dr. Katkov, for a four-month checkup. Tomorrow you will see the pediatric surgeon, and on Wednesday, you will most likely see your pediatrician for a weight check.

Last Thursday when you saw Dr. Richard Owen, the specialist in physical therapy, he examined your burned hand and expressed the belief that there most likely would be no more permanent damage. It is probable with plastic surgery that all wrist movement should return. He examined your fingers, and although the middle finger doesn't usually straighten, he felt the extender tendon was not damaged. Once the calcium deposits and edema fluid go away, the whole finger should move normally.

The wrist is now contracting upwards and not flexing down at all. I had heard from the pediatric surgeon that a brace or splint might help prevent further contraction and I urged Dr. Owen to let you have one so no further damage occurs. Later, you and I went to the Sister Kenney Occupational Therapy Department and we spent two full hours there while two young occupational therapy (OT) personnel developed what they felt would be the proper splint for your hand. I am not sure the splint is doing any good at rehabilitating the flexion movement or downward wrist motion, but it does appear to prevent further upward wrist contraction.

I have been more vigorously exercising your index and middle fingers since ten days ago when I saw the Dr. Chisholm, the pediatric surgeon who first diagnosed your hand infection several months ago. I am almost sure the swelling has gone down. It looks like the deformed shape has improved. Both doctors, Chisholm and Owen, feel the fingers will lose that lumpy swelling. Let's hope they are right!

Today you will also have a professional photographer come here to take your four-month old picture. I have been taking lots of pictures of you, alone and with Ali and Tony, but now I decided that I wanted to record your development with a series of professional photographs. I am having a terrible time deciding what you should wear—nightgown, sleeper, outfit, or dress? Well, I guess I will decide right at the last minute.

Right now, Ali and Tony are eating breakfast and you are in your infant seat on the kitchen floor watching both of them. You love to look at them and you smile for each when they play with you or glance in your direction. Ali is a big help when she rocks you to sleep in your infant seat when I am busy, especially when you are fussy or tired. Ali rocks you by sitting on the floor with the infant seat—all she does is rock it back and forth by tilting it side to side.

The big "hair raising" news occurred yesterday when I noticed that your hair had begun to fall out all over the crib bumpers and sheets. Yesterday was also a big day for eating—you consumed a grand total of twenty-six ounces of formula! Jill, my little Miss Muffet, you ate all day and were up again early this morning ready for another busy day. Well, I guess I better get going to get ready for you.

ᗒ AUGUST 6, 1981

Dear Jill,

It is early afternoon on the most gorgeous summer day. My very smiley baby is in her buggy outside in the shade. You are talking and wiggling your feet and hands while you watch and listen to everything, including the leaves rustling in the wind. Today is the only day this week that you don't have a doctor's appointment.

On Monday you saw Dr. Katkov (Dr. K), your pediatric cardiologist. He felt things were quite good. You had an EKG and a chest x-ray. Dr. K said that the EKG showed reasons why you had tachycardia attacks—something about a short atrial response or a very fast pulse in the upper chambers of the heart that, if not controlled by Lanoxin, could lead to a very rapid heartbeat. Dr. K also said that he'd like you to be about twenty pounds for your surgery, which would place your surgery somewhere between twelve and eighteen months old.

When we saw Dr. Blum, your pediatrician, yesterday, he contradicted that idea. He felt that you would only weigh about fourteen or sixteen pounds at a year. He felt you would probably have surgery at that time. My goal is to help you gain the weight you need to be strong enough for your open-heart surgery.

On Tuesday you saw Dr. Chisholm, the pediatric surgeon, and he was quite pleased with your hand. The wound is almost completely closed. There is a new kind of scab forming and it looks less "junky," although there are four little sores around your hand that have opened up to let fluid and blood out. In the past two weeks I have really exercised your fingers and I have noticed a decrease in swelling. There has also been less of a hard bump in the middle finger. The calcium seems to be disintegrating! Your wrist seems softer and more pliable.

I see Dr. Owen, the physical therapist, tomorrow afternoon. For sure we'll see if the splint that you have been wearing for one week is having any effect. Dr. Owen is quite hopeful about the return of normal hand movement. Last night, I dreamed that your hand was so beautifully healed that it didn't look any different from your other hand. Oh, but it was just a dream.

Ah, big news! Yesterday you turned over in your crib from back to front! You were asleep and got stuck on your arm. You woke up crying. I had to un-turn you, but I was delighted nonetheless. Your hair is still falling out all over your crib! Today you started solid food again and you hate it! Clearly pears and rice cereal are not your favorites on the baby menu.

Last night your favorite nurse, Debby Cloud, babysat, and you took six and a half ounces of formula from her. Then you slept for ten hours! Debby shared with me that it is such a huge reward for her when you eat well and keep it down. Her favorite part of the evening is after the other kids have gone to bed and it is very quiet in the house. She told me that you melt in her arms as if to say "Now it is just the two of us and I can relax and share my love." Truthfully, Deb adores you, and you, my precious baby, receive the very best care (with an extra special dose of love) whenever Deb helps me out at home.

Unfortunately, Jill, you developed an ear infection this past week. You had a small fever on and off since Saturday. Watching your temperature move from 99.8° to 100° was not enough of a clue to know that something was wrong. Once we all realized that you had been pulling at your ear for several days, we solved the mystery. You are now on the antibiotic Amoxicillan.

⌒ AUGUST 8, 1981

Good morning, Jill,

Today is early Saturday. You have had some applesauce and formula and have only spit up a little. Right now you are in your infant seat playing, talking to yourself and crabbing at Ali. When I was feeding you, I suddenly noticed that your middle finger on your left hand was extended just like the others. Up to this point, it was always overcurled with a large deformed bump in it. What a breakthrough! Yesterday you saw Dr. Owen again. He was quite pleased with your improvement. The wrist movement has improved greatly.

⌒ AUGUST 9, 1981

Darling Jill,

It is late at night but I just felt like writing. In the past two days I have noticed that you drink your bottles better if you are in my arms. If you are not interested in the bottle, you will act fussy. When you are ready, you will drink your bottle quickly. I wonder if this means your reflux problem is improving?

Today you ate an applesauce and cereal combination for breakfast. You appeared hungry and actually seemed to like the solid food better, although you were eager for your bottle. You then took seven ounces (but lost an ounce), took a mini-nap, and woke up to eat again later. Then for the rest of the day you ate at four-hour intervals and totaled your now-usual twenty-three ounces. You fell asleep in my arms about 9:30 P.M. while you were drinking your last bottle of the day.

⌒ AUGUST 13, 1981

Dear Jill:

So many emotions have crossed my mind in the past few days. The tears well up inside over and over again, and I struggle to keep them hidden so I don't waste a moment of time while I am enjoying you. Two days ago, a friend of mine brought her baby over to see me—a healthy seven-month-old little girl who was your same length but she weighed three pounds more. I watched this baby crawl, talk, move, and play while wondering how much you will grow and what you will be able to do in the months to come. I can't really explain my feelings. I feel so sheltered. I only want to be with you—loving you, holding you, kissing you, and making you smile. I want so desperately to cherish every moment I have with you.

I still can't believe you would ever be taken from me. I think about your open-heart surgery and I cringe at the fear that I might never hold or see my precious baby again after I kiss you good-bye at the surgery doors.

It seems incomprehensible that after all you have survived you could fail during your one crucial operation. Although I try so hard to live joyfully each day, I have this nightmare preying on my mind. I haven't slept completely through any night during the past several months.

In the meantime, when you're awake, all I do is just look at you and I melt! Your smile, your laugh, your wiggles, and your little excitements all fascinate me. I love that you are beginning to stretch your arms out to me so that I will pick you up and hold you. It is the littlest accomplishments by which I measure your success. When you hold a rattle, when you try to roll over, or even when you just sleep peacefully in your crib, I smile with joyful anticipation of your continued growth.

Your hand continues to improve. After four agonizing months, the ugly, disfiguring wound has finally closed up this week. A crusty scab, some swelling, and discoloration remain. Your fingers all curl and straighten but do not bend all the way down at the top of the knuckles. In fact, the top knuckles do not show at all. Minute sores—areas of red puffiness—can't be explained. Sometimes they ooze fluid and blood; other times they push out tiny chunks of residual calcium.

Today we go for our first occupational therapy appointment at Children's Hospital. We will be learning new exercises to bring back normal wrist and finger movement. You do have a better grasp and you hold rattles in that hand. I can even pull you up by holding both hands in mine, and best of all, you don't cry anymore during normal play with your hands.

Ah, you just woke up from a mini-nap. I do enjoy your precious smile!

⌒ AUGUST 15, 1981

Dear Jill,

I am sitting in your room on the floor while you are in your infant seat holding a rattle in your left hand. You are slowly drinking your last bottle of the night in between playing with daddy and mommy. You have been playing with the colorful crib toy that hangs across your bed.

On Thursday we saw Mary Sivaroli, the occupational therapist at Children's. Since then we have been playing with rattles and squeeze toys every spare minute to help strengthen your left hand. Mary felt that you had made great progress in the past two weeks. She gave me a sheet of exercises that you and I must do three times each day. Mostly they consist of stretching and bending your fingers and wrist. For the next eight weeks, we will go to Mary once each week for your occupational therapy. Each time your progress will be evaluated, your hand brace will be adjusted, and I will receive additional instructions for your home therapy. Already since last week, I have noticed three separate occasions when you have put a rattle from your left hand into your right and vice versa! Progress!

Lately you have had a marked increase in drooling, chewing on your fingers, blankets, and toys, and there appears to be a tiny white spot on your lower gum. I am not sure if it really is a first tooth. You seem to be tugging at your ear, so I am not sure if that is a symptom of another ear infection or of something new—teething. There is no fever, but Monday we will know for sure when we see Doctor Blum for an ear infection recheck.

Jill, you are a joy to watch and to photograph. A few days ago I took an entire roll of film as you sat in your infant seat, dressed up in a little pink flowered dress, playing, smiling, drooling, chewing on your lower lip, blowing baby bubbles, and yawning. You actually fell asleep for the final three pictures. Kodak moments that will last a lifetime.

∞ AUGUST 17, 1981

Darling Jill,

We saw Dr. Blum today. No ear infection! All the drooling and fussiness must be from teething, although, the white spot on your lower gum is not a tooth—just a white spot!

You are four-and-a-half-months old and weigh 11 pounds 9 ounces. Your hand wound has completely closed. Most of the scab is gone. There are still several red bloodlike sores and spots. When slight pressure is applied to your hand, white areas show through the translucent skin. Doctor Blum thinks it is all still large amounts of calcium that should eventually break down and dissolve. Your weight gain of a half-pound is fantastic! It must be all that rice cereal in the morning. Lastly, he checked your chest scar from the coarctation repair, but it is not completely healed.

∞ AUGUST 18, 1981

Dear Jill,

It is almost 10 P.M. Your dad is out of town for a few days. I've treasured every minute of private time with you. I can't get enough of your smiles and laughter. I love to look in your eyes and see the love that you offer when we are alone.

Tonight, you sat in your infant seat talking out loud to yourself for an hour. Happy and peaceful. Then I put you in a sitting position on the floor. You looked so tiny. But, oh, so darling! All of a sudden, you laughed and laughed—the most ever! Ali and Tony came running into the room to see what the laughter was about.

The day flew by with regular feedings, mini-naps, hand therapies, and the normal crankiness that appeared related to your constant drooling and teething action. Today the final scab on your hand fell off. Except for three little blood spots and several tiny bumps, it is completely closed and relatively smooth, albeit not beautiful by any means.

I don't know if it is wishful thinking or acute observation, but your wrist and fingers seemed more flexible tonight. You still shriek when I do your hand therapy under running water at the kitchen sink. After your wrist exercises you still require a calming period of holding, rocking, and soothing.

It still nearly kills me to hurt you when I do your hand therapy, even though I know I am doing it for your health and ultimate recovery. Some days I feel sadistic and evil because I actually enjoy doing your therapy and hand cleaning. Helping you and hurting you are inextricably linked and I must bear the dichotomy of emotions associated with that irony.

ᥱ AUGUST 20, 1981

Dear Jill,

Today we saw Mary Sivaroli, the Children's occupational therapist who designed your hand split. Mary plans your therapy and teaches me the range of motion exercises that I need to do at home. Today she added one more strap to the hand split to pull the wrist down more forcefully. She also plans to design a different splint for next week. I suppose that symbolizes progress. Mary says she is trying to pull the thumb out, away from being tucked under the other fingers. She added slightly more pressure over the middle finger, which is still swollen and deformed, to help pull it down.

I finally talked to your pediatric surgeon, Dr. Chisholm, today. He said the new skin over the wound should be moisturized with pure animal oil or lanolin. We talked about the sores that still remain. I will see him tomorrow at the Emergency Room for a checkup and review of your care.

Right now, you are sitting here just chewing on your fingers. Every once in awhile you chew on your hand brace. You seem tired. I think your occupational therapy was tough on you today. You may be tired because of all you ate today as well. This morning when you quit eating your fruit and cereal, I added the remaining portion to your bottle and you drank it right up. You need those extra calories for your growth and strength. Tonight I even added applesauce to your 5:00 bottle and pears to your 8:00 feeding. You are extremely sleepy now. Good night, little one. Rest well.

☙ AUGUST 22, 1981

Dear little Jill,

It is naptime once again. You are in your crib with your sonic teddy bear that soothes you to sleep. Yesterday we saw Dr. Chisholm at the hospital; he was pleased with the progress on your hand. The little sores are open to let the extra bits of calcium and excess fluid out of your hand—and he believes that they will eventually close. The lanolin should help smooth your skin. He said we should see some progress in the next ten days. The middle finger is straighter and no longer bulges with a big calcium bump.

I got some pictures back today of you sleeping in your infant seat. You always look so cute when you are asleep. Physically you are changing ever so slightly now. You can lie on your stomach for a few moments without crying. You also like to be pulled into a sitting position. You recognize people now and love to see your daddy, Ali, and Tony. Ali rocks you to sleep in the infant seat and Tony loves to hold and kiss you. Both kids really care about you and even Tony gets very sensitive about you. He gets upset and cries when I hurt your hand, but he is happy when he sees that it has been healing.

Lately, you get slightly "blue" when you cry for long periods or when you have put in a full day of therapy and doctors' appointments. Today, I called Dr. Katkov to mention this new sign of stress. I was told that as time goes on I would notice that your skin will appear more blue. With activity and development, there will be a greater strain on your heart resulting in the more pronounced bluish color.

Today, all three children and I walked to the grocery store. You were in your infant seat propped up in your buggy. You were wide-eyed and alert as we shopped. I left you in the checkout line for one moment while I ran back to get something. When I came back, you looked so bewildered until you saw me. Then I got the biggest, brightest smile of acknowledgement! It is moments like that that make the whole day wonderful and worth all the efforts of caring for you and worrying about your recovery and survival.

AUGUST 26, 1981

Dear Jill,

The past week has flown by with a few momentous occasions. Yesterday was the first day ever that you did not throw up! Last night you slept for twelve hours. Today you made a "b" sound for the first time so you have been cooing all kinds of "a-ba-ba-boo" sounds. Lately you cry when anyone but me holds you and you especially react when it is someone new. My favorite antic is your little arms and legs wiggling when you see your bottle, as if you are running in mid air to get it! Last Monday was your medical checkup and you weighed 11 pounds 11 ounces. Your hand wound is now all one color; only a few bumps remain.

AUGUST 28, 1981

Dear Jillsy,

Yesterday was another session of occupational therapy with Mary Sivaroli. It was a hard day for you as you cried terribly hard for one hour. Afterward you fell asleep and Mary was able to adjust your brace without upsetting you anymore. The adjustment was to cut out part of the front of the brace leaving a little piece pressing on your middle and index fingers to push them down at the top knuckle. When we returned home from the hospital I had to give you three-fourths of a tablet of phenobarbital. You slept for three hours. You really needed your rest. You were cheerful the rest of the day. During therapy you began to cry with an "mm" sound, and today you cried the same way while I did your hand. It is heartbreaking to think that you'll soon be saying "mama" when you are in pain.

⌒ AUGUST 30, 1981

My darling Jill,

Tonight I cried for the first time in weeks. While I was doing your therapy, I noticed a tiny hole in the skin of your hand that appeared to be getting larger. There may be some calcium embedded deep inside. I ran your hand under water and then touched inside the hole with the surgical tweezers. Sure enough, there was a hard calcium deposit inside, but it wouldn't come out. It only bled and the hole got bigger. Just now I looked at the open area on your hand again and it looks worse—a little bumpier and slightly reddish purple. Oh, yuck! When will it ever get better?

Ali is "baby-sitting" you again tonight while we eat dinner. Both she and Tony love to make you laugh! When you are playing with them, I see a special twinkle in your eye as you watch their every move. How terrible it would be if you didn't make it through your surgery. My concern is for Ali and Tony. Many times I cry and think about my own potential grief but then I suddenly realize how crushed the kids would be if something were to happen. They seem so sensitive and loving about you, especially Tony. When no one is watching, he talks to you so cute. He shares his little matchbox cars with you, making the "motor" sounds that make you smile. He loves to make you laugh. These past few days he has had a cold and so I kept him away from you. He was crushed.

∽ SEPTEMBER 15, 1981

Darling Jill:

It is late afternoon and you are in your infant seat watching a music box play. You are drinking your afternoon bottle, kicking your little feet and smiling away! Now you have started making little "Jillsy-bean" noises, but you keep coughing. I am not sure if it is accidental or intentional coughing spells. Things have been moving along rather well, almost without incident, during the past few weeks. Doctor checkups, polio vaccines, weight gains, the new peek-a-boo game, and out-loud laughter!

Your hand has been progressively healing. However, there are mixed opinions on whether movement and function will be restored without surgery. You don't favor one hand over the other and I am not sure if you are right-handed or a southpaw. You bring both hands together a lot and that is considered good. Last week you got another new brace for your arm. Your fingers are all even now, except for a slight bump in the middle finger. I am delighted to see that you can grasp your cradle gym ring easily with your left hand.

Now the hardest part of caring for you is your unexplained wakefulness at night. When you awaken, I feed you and cuddle you, but your fussiness can last three to four hours. Last night, you woke up every hour from 2 A.M. until 5 A.M. Yet during the day you play, talk, eat, and sleep. Of course you have your crabby period each day; I am convinced you have successfully learned to whimper and whine.

My little Jill, you love to play games now; your favorite is "peek-a-boo" where I hide your face with a cloth diaper. You laugh out loud when we play "This little piggy went to market." The big news is that you say "MA" all the time now! Your verbal repertoire consists of "ba," "boo," "abba," and now "ma." You often say "ma" when crying but I am not convinced you associate the sound with me. Lately you have refused to eat fruit and cereal so we are stopping solid foods for the time being. I will add foods to your bottle so that you still get your adequate daily intake of calories. You did gain 10 ½ ounces in just under two weeks. Speaking of food, my "little Miss Crabby" is making noises to tell me it is time to eat.

⌒ SEPTEMBER 22, 1981

Dear Jill,

It is midmorning and I just finished doing your hand therapy. It is hard to believe that the burn happened more than six months ago. We saw Mary Sivaroli last week and she felt the new brace was really helping. Your wrist flexion improved from five to fifteen degrees and you tolerate more hand manipulation during therapy without crying. I am now able to play finger games with you. Unfortunately, you still shriek during wrist-bending sessions, sending shivers up and down my spine.

Yesterday you found your feet! You reached down in your infant seat and grabbed the toes or your socks. What an accomplishment! You also like to stick out your tongue and sometimes you pull your lower lip in a sucking movement as if you are an old grandma who forgot to put in her dentures. You have no teeth yet, so this is not hard to envision.

We have all noticed an increase in your moaning and whining. Not sure of the reason, but you sit in your infant seat making constant noise. Twice now you have crabbed yourself to sleep. Your whining comes when you are tired, or full of gas, or when you want attention. In any case, it feels like we have incessant noise. My patience is waning. Even Ali and Tony tell you to quiet down.

The other day I had an incredibly crazy thought. Wouldn't it be a miracle if your heart weren't defective anymore? Wouldn't it be wonderful if there had been a terrible mistake and you didn't need open-heart surgery after all? My crazy thoughts undoubtedly reflect my decreasing ability to acknowledge that you have heart problems. You act so normal and healthy. The symptoms of abnormality—like rapid breathing, sweating, extra tiredness and minimal physical activity—all *seem* so normal, because, well, I have just grown accustomed to them.

Everyday you grow more precious to me. You are alert and lovable. My love for you and my fear of losing you have taught me to see my other children with different eyes. I love that they love each other—it is beautiful to see the feelings that they have for each other. What little loves!

∞ OCTOBER 3, 1981

Dear Jill,

You are six months old today! And, oh, what a day this was! Little Miss Super Crab. It began at 1 A.M. when you needed a bottle and Tylenol for teething and/or pain from the six-month immunization that you had yesterday. I had no ready-made bottles, so you and I made formula at that time. You threw up and were back asleep by 2:30 A.M. You were up again at 6 A.M., only to repeat the same performance. Finally I gave you a bath, but you have been restless and crabby most of the day.

Since your last nap, you seem happier and more playful. You are in your infant seat, banging a rattle and making incredible noises. You are talking, smiling, and blowing little bubbles with your mouth (we call them raspberries). Now it sounds like you are singing opera! You have been playing so much lately that your breathing is slightly labored. When you give off little grunts it reminds me that your heart is defective and your lungs can't handle the added activity of your growth.

Speaking of growth, you weighed 13 pounds 2 ounces at your checkup the other day. You have grown a total of four inches since birth and are now 26 ½ inches long. You had your DPT shot, although they only gave you a half-dose, and your oral polio vaccine. Dr. Blum encouraged me to work with you to aid in strengthening your back and leg muscles. I have noticed that you don't use any of these muscles on your own to further your development. You also don't like to be turned on your tummy, so you have made no attempt to creep or crawl.

I did work with you several times today to encourage muscle development. I had you in the walker and we played floor games. I held you in my lap to get you to sit up, and one time I even held you up under your arms, hoping you would bear some weight on your legs. Finally tonight you did! When I saw you straighten your legs, I almost cried. And when I said, "Good girl —I am so proud of you," you smiled as if you really knew just how I felt.

⌒ OCTOBER 6, 1981

Dearest Jill,

It is 9:30 P.M. and you, my precious darling, are sound asleep in your crib, nose to nose with your little sonic Teddy Bear. It was a long day for you.

After several bottles, three naps, and therapy sessions, you played in your walker before we had to leave to see Dr. Owen at Sister Kenney Institute and then Dr. Chisholm at Children's Medical Center. While we were gone, you ate again and fell asleep in the car on the way home. You slept until 5 P.M. and then it took you a full two hours to drink another bottle. I finally put you in bed for the night at 8 P.M.

My horoscope in today's newspaper was so strange because it actually described how I feel about you right now: "Period of brooding is only temporary. Feelings of discouragement will pass soon." How appropriate it seems because I have become saddened about your growth and development. It hurts me terribly to see my beautiful, bright, baby daughter begin to lag behind developmentally.

I guess it hit me on Saturday when you turned six months old. All you can really do is roll side-to-side, play on your back, or sit in your infant seat. My heart ached for you, not really for me, because I feel you want to do so much more. Jill, you try to sit up in your infant seat over and over again, but you can't. I talked to two doctors about your development and I was told that I must actively help you strengthen and develop your muscles so you can begin to use your back and leg muscles for sitting, creeping, crawling, and ultimately standing.

Just when I thought things were getting so easy, things changed and got harder all over again. Everything with you is totally mommy-related; my total input goes to helping you live, grow, develop and thrive. It really gets to me sometimes.

Then I think of the people whose babies will never be alert or physically functional and I get angry with myself for being the least bit depressed. What right do I have to be sad about your slowness when it is only temporary? Yet the fear of surgery hangs over our heads.

Today Dr. Chisholm dealt me another blow. He said it would be three full years before we could quit using the Lanolin cream on your hand. I never realized how terribly long the healing process is. Fear grips and gnaws at me every time I think about your open-heart surgery and all the IVs that will be placed in your body. I get scared at the thought of any further damage to your skin from another chemical burn. To shake off these ominous thoughts, I just reflected back on the doctors' reports we received today. Both Dr. Chisholm and Dr. Owen were pleased with the progress of your hand and they told me to continue with four more weeks of occupational therapy. Every day I talk myself into holding onto the moment and living with the daily progress that is taking place. It's a way of finding peace.

○ OCTOBER 9, 1981

Dear Jill,

It is midmorning and I have just spent the last hour crying terribly and holding you, saying over and over: "Please, little baby, don't let anything else be wrong—I just couldn't take it!" Jill, you were developmentally assessed by the Children's Hospital occupational therapist yesterday. During the exam, Mary commented that you arched your back and stiffened your body several times during play and when you got tired.

I called Dr. Blum, who was surprised to hear that you did this. He explained to me that Mary's concern might reflect her fear that you could have possibly suffered brain damage when you were oxygen-deprived during a heart arrest episode in your early days. This is all guesswork at this point. There is no conclusive proof that anything is wrong, but your behavior is different and needs explaining. My own heart is heavy at the notion that this may be a serious problem. I just couldn't bear the idea that you are brain-damaged and I refuse to consider the possibility except with tears of desperation.

Dr. Blum will be calling Mary today to review her assessment but he is already suggesting that a neurologist, Dr. Roger McCormick, conduct a complete neurological workup and full assessment. Needless to say, I am just sick about this newest development. My precious, bright, and beautiful child, who seemed so perfect except for her heart and burned hand, may have another major flaw.

○ SATURDAY, OCTOBER 10, 1981

Dear Jill,

It is 10 P.M. and I am still swirling in a state of disbelief. Your dad has gone to bed and there is no one to talk to. I am left alone with my thoughts. I talked with Dr. Blum twice on Friday and he had called Mary Sivaroli to discuss your developmental assessment. Basically, it seems that Mary must have told him several observations that made him curious. Dr. Blum called them "soft signs" or symptoms that could be explained any number of different ways. The signs that Mary observed included your arched back and stiff extended body, and your tight knees and legs that were reluctant to relax during a sitting exercise. It appears you don't want to or can't move. In fact, you have spent so much time lying only on your back that you have worn your hair thin in one spot.

It is apparent that you can't sit up, stand, or use your legs as the average baby your age does. But the question is why? Is your heart making your energy-deficient, or do you lack the muscle coordination to succeed? Or worse yet, are you physically unable to because of defective mechanisms in your brain? In my heart, I believe that you will get stronger every day and you will achieve even minute goals if I work with you and coach your development along. I personally don't see the stiff legs if you are relaxed and not overly tired. I only feel the arched back as an action related to several things: playfulness (you do it with a smile and throw your head back and pull yourself up as you are doing it); cramping (you scream and arch together as if you have cramps or gas pains); and temper (one of your nurses commented that she had seen other babies do this as part of a temper tantrum). All of that makes sense to me for when you get tired or crabby, you moan and arch into your extended stiffness.

Call it mother's intuition (or a mother's refusal to face facts), but I just can't believe that any part of your brain was affected from your earlier cardiac arrests. As you sleep, finally, I watch your tender face, and at moments like this, I push away any thought that there is anything else wrong with you, my child. Rest well, my little one. Whatever happens, I will be there with you.

⌒ OCTOBER 14, 1981

Dear Jill,

The past two days have been among the most difficult that I have had to endure in many months. Yesterday I had my appointment with Dr. Roger McCormick, a pediatric neurologist, who confirmed the suspicions that you might have suffered some sort of brain damage during your critical first few days of life.

His impressions and opinions were not based on clinical proof, but only on judgments made during a physical exam. He felt that most likely there had been some mild damage to the brain function relating to your gross-motor coordination. You are slow to develop normal physical accomplishments like sitting, balance, and good back and head control. Your legs become tight in a sitting position and you can't support yourself in that position. He said that your back-arching and hyperextension is an inappropriate behavior that interferes with normal development. Your arching works against your ability to balance.

I don't understand everything that was said to me yesterday. I met with Dr. McCormick's nurse for forty-five minutes and then with the doctor himself for an hour or so. He was overly patient with me, answered all my questions, and tried to prepare me for what lies ahead. He tried to paint a hopeful picture of how, with therapy, your development will improve with time. Unfortunately, he shocked me severely when he diagnosed your problem as cerebral palsy and then used terms like "spastic" to describe your condition and lack of coordination.

I drove home in the pouring rain with tears streaming down my face and your innocent little eyes glaring at me. Anger has been bubbling under the surface since I saw Dr. McCormick and despite the fact I want to wish it all way, I hate him and all other doctors for their inability to fix it or prevent it from happening in the first place. What's worse are my own inept feelings when I glance at my precious baby, the sweet, unsuspecting victim of all of this heartache.

Today I spent an hour-and-a-half at therapy with you, talking to Mary Sivaroli about your development, the assessment, therapy, and your future. Mary, with all her sensitivity and caring, patiently explained that she will be in charge of helping you through Dr. McCormick's care. She wrote me two full pages of exercises for developmental therapy and explained how every normal movement will be broken down into minute steps that we will teach you to do. It was amazing to see how normal physical movements can be reduced to step-by-step components that build up a complete action. I will work with you diligently and try to keep a record of what we do and how you progress. Maybe then I can get a better feeling for how our therapy is improving your development.

At home, I worked with you doing a series of your physical exercises. We played with the ball in a sitting position for about ten minutes. You also sat in the high chair for ten minutes and we did a leg massage with the bicycle motion two times. I practiced placing your toes to your mouth—a stability exercise that prepares you for sitting in a balanced position and I sewed little bells on your socks so that when you play on your back and raise your feet in the air, the bells will draw attention to your toes— again stretching your development toward a more balanced position. Whenever you arched your back and stiffened up, I stopped the exercise immediately or changed the position.

The next goal in play therapy is to get you to stretch out your arms when we play with a beach ball or when we place you on a pillow for balance and support. I also tried to have you kick at things. None of these exercises were successful. I was not totally discouraged, however, because you can roll back and forth unassisted!

Jill, you love your high chair! You will sit very straight in it for about fifteen minutes. You pulled up to a sitting position for me today and you put you hands out front on your toes. All in all, we worked hard today on the step-by-step exercises that should help you develop.

ᖇ OCTOBER 16, 1981

Dear Jill,

Today is your picture day! You have already turned over five times today from back to front—easily! Your arm came out from under you and you lifted your head way up! You even reached out for toys! You sat in your high chair for thirty to forty minutes and we had an extended playtime with the exercise ball tonight. For the very first time, you pushed it with your feet and you played a rolling ball game with Ali too. While you sat on the floor, I tried to push your knees down to help you relax; you sat forward, reached out for the ball, and placed your hands on your toes and the floor. Then you pushed the ball to Ali or tried to get the ball from Ali. Looking back now, these baby-steps of progress seemed huge! It was a good day.

ᖇ OCTOBER 19, 1981

Darling Jill,

It is 7:30 P.M. and you are sound asleep on the floor of your room...on your tummy! You were so sleepy tonight that while I was taking my bath, I let you play on the floor of my bedroom right near me. All of a sudden it seemed so quiet. Ali went to check on you and found you asleep right in the middle of the floor with your head on a diaper. She said you looked just precious.

Today was your first day of developmental therapy with Mary Sivaroli. We went through the two pages of exercises, plus some new things using the beach ball, slant board, roller, and mirror. Mary saw some progress, as did I, mostly in head control and sitting balance. You are relaxing your legs slowly and as you do, you are doing better. You are putting your hands down a little as you sit, thus gaining better balance and support for yourself. It was really good to see your progress—no matter how slight, it makes it so much easier to face each day with a positive attitude.

It's so frustrating to know that what most babies assimilate naturally or instinctively, you have to be *taught*, one step at a time. I hate it and hate the frustration of knowing how far we have to go, but whenever I see any sign of progress, like I did today, I find it so much easier to look at the bright side of life and not dwell on the pain.

The hardest part of today was thinking about your speech development. You began to say "dada." You even repeated it a lot after I said it to you. This should have made me happy, but instead I felt scared and depressed. Your speech doesn't sound clear or crisp. As I watched your tongue say the "da" sound, it looked sort of curled instead of flat against the roof of your mouth. Years ago when I was in undergraduate school majoring in elementary education, I did an in-depth study of language development and analyzed Ali's language progression of speech for many months. Knowing the relationship between sound acquisition and the role of the tongue on word formation gave me insight into watching your vocabulary development. You make a lot of sounds like "dada," "baba," "gaga," and "nana," but I just can't get over the fear that your speech won't be clearly understandable. I pray that I am wrong.

ᜃ OCTOBER 23, 1981

Darling Jill,

Things have settled down quite a bit during these last few days. I am not as intense in my all-out effort to cure you all at once. I still do your developmental exercises, but I am not as consumed with getting you to grow and develop. We continue to do the sitting exercises every day. You also practice rolling the ball with Ali and Tony; we sewed more bells on your baby socks so that you continue to reach for your toes. You sit in the high chair two times each day. We practice several different movement exercises daily—all disguised as play-games. We kick at a box, sway side-to-side, roll over a ball, and finally end with leg massages. You stiffen when I massage your thighs—you even arched your back and stiffened once while lying down. You relax better during the sitting ball games, and once you even put your own hand down to support yourself to gain balance.

Jill, you pull to a sitting position easily now, but your legs do not open up into the natural tripod position of balance. You do not seem relaxed when you are sitting up. Your days are still full with eating, naps, and play therapy. Sometimes you actually play on the floor by yourself in the infant seat, or in the high chair. And most of the time, you will play by yourself when you first wake up from a nap.

Unfortunately, you are still waking up or crying in your sleep several times each night. You get yourself stuck in the corner of the crib, wedged against the bumpers. You cry until someone rescues you. Last night you repeated this unconscious ritual four times. Finally, I turned on your little sonic bear to quiet you down and lull you back to sleep.

And now, as I close my eyes for the night, I am grateful for the week's end. It has been a trying, difficult, and emotionally draining week. Bless the quiet of the night.

⌒ OCTOBER 26, 1981

Dear Jill,

It is five o'clock on Monday morning. Ugh. A half hour ago, you woke me up by crying in your sleep. You rolled onto your tummy, and then discovered that you couldn't turn back. Once I rescued you, you went back to sleep but I was fully awake and deep in thought.

Your dad and I have decided to buy a new house. We have looked for a while but haven't found "the perfect one." I believe that your dad wants to purchase a very large, prestigious home and I certainly want more space so that you children will each have your own room and a large family room to play in. Part of me believes that a larger home will bring more tranquility to the marriage. I often think that if your dad had more space to be alone our interactions and relationship would improve.

So, I have been energetically thinking about buying a new house and selling this one. I have been extra busy getting our house ready for real estate showings and still managing your care and doctors' appointments.

I am taking you to therapy today. Mary and I will assess what exercises we do so we can make an evaluation of your progress. It is amazing how every little movement for natural physical development is broken down into minute tasks—and these little movements result in a normal activity like sitting up and balancing without falling over.

Jillsy, your progress is encouraging. I can easily pull you to a sitting position, but usually you are not relaxed enough to balance alone. Your best relaxation comes by playing with the ball or when I place a "busy box" in front of you. Only then do you relax and get busy!

This past weekend, you seemed to be fighting a cold and consequently were overtired and cranky. I noticed more arching of your back during normal activities and more crying. The exciting development was a scoot forward from a position on all fours. It wasn't exactly crawling, but it was fun to think it was a distant cousin or predecessor. When you are on your tummy you try to bend your knees up. They scoot up and straighten, but you don't actually go anywhere...yet.

∽ NOVEMBER 1, 1981

Good morning, Jillsy,

It is Sunday morning and you are just waking up. It has been such a terribly hectic week that I have had no time to record the events of your progress or our lives. Daddy and I bought a new house! It is very large and on a prestigious lake parkway in

Minneapolis. It was a huge decision that promises to be a big event in our lives.

In the last three weeks we have been working with a kitchen designer, heating contractor, and the real estate people in preparation for moving and selling our existing home. Grandma Phyl has been babysitting for you three consecutive Thursdays from midmorning until six o'clock. The break away from our daily routine has been wonderful since you know your Grandma and love to be with her.

Anyway, all of my spare time is devoted to the house—cleaning and planning. I have been too tired to record in this diary. Let's see if I can catch up on missing events. Last Monday, you saw Dr. Katkov for your six-and-half-month checkup. Your weight was 13 pounds 13 ½ ounces. The status of your heart was the same as in previous exams. The x-rays showed no change and your color remains good. Dr. K questions the diagnosis of mild cerebral palsy based on the fact many cyanotic heart disease babies have developmental delay. Dr. K would like to postpone your open-heart surgery until twelve to eighteen months, if possible. He would like you to be closer to twenty pounds. The plan is to have all of your doctors, (Dr. K, Dr. Singh, Dr. Blum, Dr. Helseth, and maybe Dr. McCormick) meet with your dad and me to discuss the surgical procedures, possible complications, and what exactly might take place during the open-heart operation.

From a developmental perspective: Jill, you saw Mary Sivaroli the past two Mondays. You will see Dr. Owen at Sister Kenney Institute tomorrow.

MONDAY EVENING, NOVEMBER 2, 1981

Jillsy,

Today Mary saw significant progress. You can remain in an unsupported sitting posture for longer periods (many seconds). Sometimes you spontaneously put your hands forward on your toes or the floor and you breathe much easier during the sitting exercises. I think you are actually enjoying that position! Mary said that you have better head and trunk control and appear to be arching your back less. You still arch when you get angry or uncomfortable or tired.

We noticed how well you sit in my lap—unsupported now! You may sit for several minutes at a time. While this is not the same as sitting flat on the floor unassisted, it still demonstrates an improved control of head and body. Jill, you used both hands equally today. You reached for objects with both hands while you were stretched over the beach ball during exercises. We don't know why but you were also cranky and quite temperamental today. Your left leg was much more relaxed than the right one, but the right did straighten and loosen up more today.

After your therapy session, Mary walked with us to Dr. Owens' office where she discussed your hand progress with him. He feels we should maintain the flexion we achieved by using a static night splint. He wants me to continue your range of motion exercises two to three times per day and other than that, I can let you develop your wrist naturally with active play. When asked, he couldn't answer whether the total flexion would return. Dr. Owens didn't know that you saw Dr. McCormick, but he felt that whatever brain damage you may have suffered was very mild in light of the progress that you have made in the past month. Music to my ears! I still refuse to believe you have suffered *any* brain damage.

At the end of the session Dr. Owens held you up to see if your legs hung down normally...and they did! This is an indication that you should be able to walk properly without the "cross over" leg look. I pray that is true. When I think about it, I pray that you, my precious baby girl, will never look, act, or move in a way that would ever cause anyone to make fun of you.

ᴄᴏ NOVEMBER 3, 1981

Dear Jill,

Seven months old today! Weight 13 pounds 10 ½ ounces and 27 inches long. It appears that you have lost weight since your weigh-in at Dr. K's on October 26. Well, the truth is, you threw up five times this morning before your appointment at Dr. Blum's. That was the bad news. The good news is, you rolled over and lifted your head up high while he examined you. You sat alone for a few seconds for him too. You also placed your left hand down for support several times while sitting. You are spontaneously placing your hands forward more often and sitting more normally each time.

ᴄᴏ NOVEMBER 6, 1981

Dear Jill,

While your physical progress continues, you have had an ear infection and are on Amoxicillian for ten days. You have been cranky most of the last few days and while we have been using nose drops, cough syrup, vaporizers, and the antibiotic, you have hardly slept at all. Finally, yesterday, you were better although you continued to cough.

Today was a red-letter day though! You actually smiled at the baby in the mirror and sat unsupported for fifteen seconds! What small miracles. You are now rolling easily onto your tummy and slept most of the night in that position.

The other big news is the constant chatter. "Da-Da," "Ba," "Ga," "Na" and "La." You haven't said "ma" yet, though. We did more exercises on the floor today. You "walked" to a paper cup with the wheel barrel exercise and you did very well reaching out with both hands to retrieve the cup. You placed both hands on the floor with your fingers spread apart normally and you appear to be putting equal pressure on both hands.

My best news of all today is that you sat all by yourself—time and again—for a few minutes each time. Progress…tiny but big!

 NOVEMBER 9, 1981

Jill,

You waved "bye-bye" today. You love the baby in the mirror and you sat unassisted for five minutes today without support. Your weight was 14 pounds 2 ounces.

 NOVEMBER 17, 1981

Dear Jill,

Yesterday you had OT with Mary Sivaroli. You had a very good session. You were sitting up for extended periods of time, balancing better, finding hidden objects, lying on your tummy without crying and trying to do new exercises. In fact, you were crying less and smiling more throughout the entire session. Your sitting has improved so drastically (you can sit for about fifteen minutes at a time) and you will normally use your hands for support at your side or in front to keep your balance.

As of yesterday, we have begun work on building toward crawling. We are using a roll of support under your chest when you are on your tummy. We can encourage you to lift one hand to reach a toy and then to support yourself with the other hand. We just tried this and it worked well. I am continually amazed at the minute steps we must use to break normal physical movements down so you can be "taught" how to develop. You are beginning to prop yourself on your hands and you don't seem to mind being on your stomach.

Paper cups and paper are among your favorite toys now. You talk much of the time with words like "Da," "ah," "ga" and a few "mmmm" sounds, but no "ma" as of yet. Last but not least,

Jill, you are drooling all the time. There are no teeth yet, but it appears they are in progress.

⌒ NOVEMBER 24, 1981

Dear Jill,

Next week you will be eight months old. It is hard to believe. It is even harder to believe that we could ever lose you now that you are so embedded in our lives. You now have regular play-times with Ali and Tony. Just yesterday Tony was reading you *Hop on Pop*, a Dr. Seuss book, and you loved listening to him. I also let you sit in their beds with them once in awhile and I know they love having you snuggle. Ali, being older and more responsible, gets to hold you in her lap. I took a picture of the two of you when smiling and looking at each other. You have become much more a part of their lives.

However, when I try and envision the future, I only see you as a baby. I am not sure what that means. In my mind's eye, I cannot picture you as a little girl or even a toddler.

You have started coughing again. I have you on cough medicine and the vaporizer. Once again I spent the night on the floor of your room after feeding you a bottle in the middle of the night. Of course, you spit up the contents of the bottle all over yourself and your bed, but not enough to know if you are really sick. Forgetting that you are not feeling well, the good news is that you are waving bye-bye and hi now…but only when YOU want to! You wiggle and gets so excited whenever you see Ali and Tony because you absolutely adore them!

I did your new physical exercises every other day last week. You are doing okay. There is no drastic change except that I am noticing that you support your weight on your legs more often for brief periods of time. That really is an improvement since you *never* put weight on your legs before. In fact, you didn't even put them down to the floor before.

We also saw Dr. Chisholm today but, unfortunately, there was no further improvement in your hand. He was optimistic about further recovery *if* we continue working hard at the flexion exercises. By bending your hand and stretching your wrist, he believes we can make further progress. I get chills thinking of his instructions—I must push your wrist down farther three times a day instead of just once. I need to make sure I use the Lanolin and rub it deeply into your skin. He feels this is the only way to aid the stretching of the scar tissue. It really is ugly, but by now I am becoming almost immune to the taut, dark, glossy scar.

∽ NOVEMBER 25, 1981

Dearest Jill,

I have just put my very tired baby to bed. Today has been a long day. You were up at four o'clock in the morning; you cried on and off for much of the day. At one point, you drank eight ounces, which was wonderful! Surprisingly, there was no throwing up! We went over to our new house (an exciting venture) where you napped in your playpen for the afternoon. You also played on the floor and then fell back asleep in the car on the way home to the old house. Once home, it was a normal and routine day with feedings every two to three hours. But the fun thing of the day was the fact that you waved bye-bye all day! You loved your new skill. What fun for the rest of us.

We own two homes right now because we want to fix up the new one before moving in. We are remodeling the kitchen, breakfast room, and large playroom for you three kids. Your dad has orchestrated the different work crews who are also installing a security system, updating the heating and air conditioning, and improving other mechanical functions. I like to stay involved, too, so whenever I can, while Ali and Tony are in school, I take you there with me to look around. The playpen and other baby things that I have left there make it easier to travel back and forth.

Developmentally, the exercises that we are concentrating on are pivoting on the stomach and moving around to reach toys that are farther away. I am also placing toys slightly off to the side while you are in a sitting position so that you must pivot or turn to reach them. The doctors want me to encourage the "four-point" position of knees and hands on the floor; I do this by rolling you over a foam roller. Another exercise includes sitting with your feet directly on the floor to encourage better sitting balance and to experience the tactile feel of your feet actually touching the floor.

⌒ NOVEMBER 27, 1981

Dear precious little baby:

Yesterday I cried several times from a deep heartache of the knowledge that you could die within the year. Yesterday was Thanksgiving Day and I did a very poor job of being thankful for what I had because I was so scared at the thought that I might lose you. Will you be with us next year for the Thanksgiving celebration?

You are so sweet and precious to me. Today I watched you sleep in the car all the way to the hospital for therapy. You looked so angelic and dear. I do love you so. I hate hurting you with the hand therapy—I only want to hold you and love you more.

I think you have another cold. I think we got this one together! You were very crabby at therapy today, although you accomplished a lot. When we got home, you had a bottle, went to sleep right away and slept soundly for two hours. You just woke up and are watching me write in your journal to record the activities at therapy today.

Jill, you pivoted on your tummy about one-hundred-eighty degrees. You supported yourself much better and you clearly lifted yourself way up on your hands and knees. Once you were in a crawling position, you reached forward two times supporting yourself on hands and feet—not knees! Not sure of the meaning of this progress but it was considered good.

MONDAY, NOVEMBER 30, 1981

Dear Jill,

We saw Dr. Blum today. You weighed 14 pounds 10 ounces and you were almost 28 inches long. I wish I could accurately describe my feelings lately. It's as if you are my closest and most important relation and whenever I am away from you, I miss you so much. My adult friends don't seem to mean anything to me. It is like no one really understands my life. And it's not that my life is so bad—in fact, I truly love being with you.

No one can really understand how totally involved I get with you. There I was at a hockey game with your dad, crying to myself because I started imagining what it would be like to say good-bye to you at the time of your open-heart surgery. It is so overwhelming and frightening to imagine a last night with my baby. "Our" baby for that matter. I know it will be just as hard on your dad to imagine that night, especially since I will probably stay with you in the hospital and he will be at home alone with Ali and Tony.

Sometimes I feel so sheltered and closeminded. It is hard to imagine doing anything but taking care of you, my little love. In some ways, your situation allows me to love and appreciate Ali and Tony even more. But at the same time I feel so pulled, like I don't have enough time for all of you.

The good part is that you adore them. You look for them and get so very excited to see them. Your legs wiggle and you smile from ear to ear when they come into view. Ali and Tony both held the bottle for you today. I never used to let them feed you because of your digestive problems. Ali holds you a little, carries you, sits you up, and lays you down. She "babysits" almost every night in our family room/den while your dad and I have dinner in the other room. Tonight you and I were in the den after the other children had gone to bed. You "pivoted" your hands off to one side from a sitting position several times and you pulled yourself to stand while I held your hands.

⌒ DECEMBER 3, 1981

Dear Jill,

You are eight months old today. Tonight you did several new things for the first time, including playing on the den floor, sitting and leaning forward and to the side. You reached over the side and then fell onto your tummy, but recovered quickly by rolling onto your back, onto your tummy and then onto your back again. It was almost like a game. But just now, as I write this, you fell completely backwards! You almost started to cry but now you're talking to yourself and rolling over. You are extremely tired, but very playful and talkative.

⌒ DECEMBER 6, 1981

Dear Jill,

You saw Dr. Farber at Fairview Southdale Hospital today. Your fever was 100.8°, an hour *after* Tylenol. Fevers in "heart babies" are more worrisome. Your symptoms were extra crabbiness and an incredibly drippy nose. Your eyes were clear, but your throat was quite red, so the doctor did a culture for strep throat and a blood count to determine if there was a bacterial infection. The blood count showed an elevated white count, so Dr. Farber put you on an antibiotic. You just had your first dose and you took it quite well. You are now sitting in the middle of my bed playing with your pink basket of toys. You are getting quite good at reaching the toys you want while you are in a sitting position. You can lean all the way forward; you can put both hands down and reach off to the side. Sometimes, you lean all the way down, almost to your tummy and then you pull back up again. Every small movement is so exaggerated in my mind...but it is progress. I pay attention to and relish every little accomplishment that symbolizes normal development.

⌾ DECEMBER 8, 1981

Dear Jillsy,

It is 10:30 P.M. I just got home from an evening out, and you are sound asleep. I had to peek at you right away. You look adorable and precious in your crib. Your nurse, Debby, babysat for you tonight. You needed cough syrup, Lanoxin, and your antibiotic.

When Deb arrived, she mirrored all of my feelings about how you take your medicine. First of all, you know when I put it in your bottle and you won't drink it. You won't take it from a syringe dropper or from a little rubber nipple that I put near your mouth to suck from. Taking medicine is a full-blown affair and Debby got quite a kick out of my overreaction to the comical but frustrating sequence of events.

Okay, now for the fun stuff. Jillsy, you are giving kisses! This started about two weeks ago but you have really perfected it lately. You give a kiss with your mouth wide open, placed on my cheek. You are so loving. Major progress in the game department: You finally learned how to play "How big is the baby?" Today you banged two toys together to make noise and loved it! You use the toys to hit the table or whatever you can find to make noise. And the best news of all—your left arm is beginning to pick up movement all the time. I loved that. And I love you!

∞ DECEMBER 9, 1981

My sweet, precious little girl,

You started crying at midnight and didn't stop for two hours. The tears ceased only after you and I camped out on the floor of your room together with three pillows and two blankets between us. You either had a bad dream or stomach cramps because you gave bloodcurdling screams that just wouldn't quit until I calmed you down with gentle rocking. You need your sleep because you have OT motor skill testing tomorrow. There will be cognitive skill tests, too, and I am hoping for good results on everything.

∞ DECEMBER 11, 1981

Dear Jill,

Here it is late in the evening and whenever I sit down to reminisce for this diary, only the developmental victories and problems come easily to mind. So often during the course of a day of caring for you, fleeting emotions come to mind and I tear up with a loving, emotional feeling of anticipation.

Just yesterday, when I was bathing you in the big bathtub for the first time (before I always used the kitchen sink because it was easier to support you), I sat there with a feeling of tranquility and a new patience. It was an ideal feeling, one I wish I could have had with all of my children all of the time. What I discovered, however, is that I was savoring a moment in time. That is a magnificent feat for me. But in this case, I was savoring every moment as if it will be the last. For once, I wasn't yelling and rushing through the mundane motions of everyday life. With you, Jill, more than with Ali or Tony, I marvel at your every expression, movement, sound, and accomplishment.

Perhaps time has faded my memory somewhat, and Ali and Tony use to melt my heart in the same way. I have a tendency to be self-deprecating, so it is possible that I truly reveled in each miniscule accomplishment of my first two children but don't give myself credit for that now. Having you has helped me to search for the goodness and loving in all of my children and to appreciate the miniscule moments.

Some days when I am totally enmeshed in your development and every joyous accomplishment, I condemn myself for not praising my other children during their formative development years. I must say that having you in my life has helped me to openly express my love for my other children more often.

Sometimes I find myself just staring at Ali and Tony, realizing what good children they really are. Then I want to hug them and grab them, and keep them young forever. And with you—I am starting to be overwhelmed by the swift passing of your infancy. At eight months, you have completed two-thirds of your first year. When I think how slowly time really passes and how far you have come, I get frustrated because, in reality, those terribly long, hard days whizzed by and your first six months are gone.

It's hard to believe I used to hate waking up in the morning to feed you. Those early morning hours were so long and treacherous—hours of feeding and refeeding the same bottle. But now I love waking up and looking at you. I find myself watching you sleep, no matter where you may be—in the car or in your crib. I just keep staring at your angelic face. There is a softness and tenderness to your little pink cheeks that have become indelibly printed in my mind.

Your daily routine is still filled with developmental tasks; even games like pat-a-cake have become monumental accomplishments for us. Last night you placed one hand on top of the other in an effort to mimic me. Just that slight maneuver was a glorious moment.

We are still working on pulling you up to a sitting position and then to stand. Today you retrieved a toy in your crib that you wanted to play with. You also fell over sideways from a sitting position and landed on your tummy twice. The third time I caught you and helped you with a soft landing! Today you were in the kitchen and had your hands out in front of you and then off to the side when you slipped farther and farther forward. You ultimately landed on your stomach by yourself. Knowing that we have developed range-of-motion methods for teaching you these basic physical movements, I am acutely aware of each step of your development. A twist and turn, the placement of your hand down or a motion forward—everything is seen as progress.

You sleep on your stomach most of the time now and even scoot backwards in your crib while on your tummy. Your little legs come poking through the bars of your bed many times during the night. I love to go into your room and find you wherever you have landed in the course of your slumber.

☙ DECEMBER 20, 1981

Dear Jillsy,

We had OT developmental testing today. Your age is eight months and one week. You tested at nine months cognitive development and seven months physical/motor development. You are beginning to learn pat-a-cake by putting one hand on the other—always right on left. You can turn from sitting into almost a crawl. You place two hands on the floor, bending one leg behind yourself and then stretching forward to reach a toy. However, you do not go all the way forward onto all fours and are not yet supporting a full crawling position.

Our daily games include "This little piggy went to market" and "Bam-Bam," a game that your daddy invented. The game consists of banging your little hand on Daddy, a table, or any other convenient surface at the sound of the command "Bam-Bam." The best fun of all is when you get excited. You wiggle your legs back and forth and practically shake all over with excitement! But for whatever reason lately, you have been crying yourself to sleep at night.

☞ DECEMBER 29, 1981

My dear Jill,

It has taken me days to finally sit down and write in your diary and yet there have been so many moments in the past week that I have wanted to stop everything and just sit down to record my feelings.

It is now ten o'clock. You are finally asleep after crying on and off since eight o'clock. Sometimes I wonder how much you hate going to bed because it means being away from the people who love you. In the last week you have really warmed up to your dad. You seem to adore playing with him and likewise he with you. You have your own games where he makes you smile a great big "Jill" smile or he blows on your hand and you laugh out loud.

I think you make your dad feel vulnerable—a position that he, as a controlling and dominant person, doesn't easily accept. He has identified with your survivor abilities. Ever since your early days when you were so very sick and beat the odds in your early surgeries, he has acknowledged that you are just like him— strong and determined. But now I see his emotions on his face when you respond to him during play or quiet time together. On Christmas Day you sat with him for a long time opening presents. Two days later he baby-sat with you while I took Ali and Tony to the movies, and one night he even woke you up to play in front of his secretary who came over to visit. Pride was written all over his face. He really misses you when he works late, and you love to see him, except in the morning when you have the "hungry crabbies" and you know that Mommy's got the bottle!

Lately, Jill, you are getting "nosey!" It is really so cute to watch you watch us. You keep your wide eyes glued to whoever runs in and out of the room that you are in. If someone makes a noise, you perk up to see what's going on, and you will even strain to watch Ali or Tony when they go out of sight. As for myself, I cannot stop watching you! I am afraid that I will run out of time loving you.

⌒ DECEMBER 30, 1981

Darling Jill,

It is late afternoon and you are playing on the floor with your toys. You are sort of talking to yourself, playfully avoiding an overdue nap. While "dada" is your prime word, you have many new sounds that have developed in the last few weeks. Most of them are indecipherable to me, but they appear to mean something to you. You say them with such conviction! The only one I pretend to understand is "goo-gi" which comes out in the exact tone as I use when I say "Good girl." Of course, I must repeat those words to you fifty times each day!

You understand more every day. I can teach you new things all the time and it is fun to see you explore, copy, seek out and try. You'll say "da" when I say "dolly" and you will even give your dolly a kiss on command. This afternoon, you finally kissed the baby in the mirror for the first time. You still play pat-a-cake, right hand on the left, and you can bang two blocks together the same way—right on left. However, yesterday at therapy you began pulling the left hand in almost an exact manner as the right. It seems mundane, but considering that your left hand was "frozen" in a permanent disfigured position just months ago, this is BIG progress.

On Monday, December 28, you saw Dr. Owen at Sister Kenney Institute for an evaluation. Basically, the report was good. He felt that the left hand had improved from a twenty-degree flexion to thirty-five degrees. Your scar is either smooth or coarse looking, depending on the amount of lanolin that is applied and the frequency of the application. The left hand looks normal in color and size when, compared to the right, but then again, it can have a purple tinge to it. There is no way one could call it normal or healed.

Jill, you use your left hand normally, though, and have for several months. However, you appear to have a preference for your right hand. Who knows if that is your natural inclination or a strength deficit due to the burn and injury? We will see Dr. Owen again in two months.

⌒ JANUARY 1, 1982

My dearest Jill:

My New Year's wish for you, precious one, is that 1982 will bring you the miracle of life and you will survive your open-heart surgery. May our love bring you through whatever lies ahead.

It is now 9 P.M. and I just rocked you back to sleep in my arms after you woke up suddenly from a sound sleep. I find it so hard to believe you are almost nine months old. I want to keep you little and love you for as long as I can.

I keep thinking how fast time has gone in these past months, but then I find it so hard to believe how far we have come. The days of colic and screaming and excessive throwing up are so far behind us. But when I do your hand exercises each day, I still feel the same hate and disgust that I always have until I think how much your arm has improved. It is hard to believe as I fight to press your little wrist downward that there was ever a time that it would not move at all. Tonight your dad watched me move it and we saw how easily the wrist goes up and down in a sort of gentle "bye-bye" motion. Without any pressure from me there is limited range of motion, but with extreme force I can bend your hand down to almost thirty-five degrees of flexion just like Dr. Owen measured the last time we were there. What amazes me is how the burn scar never seemed to grow with you. Instead, it became a smaller percentage of your total arm as you grew. The ugly purplish-red glassy scar used to be about half the length of your arm.

Tonight I quickly practiced two of your developmental exercises and to my delight you did two things you had not done before! First, while lying over a foam rubber exercise roll that supported your chest, you held yourself up on your arms. Then when I bent your knees up underneath you into a crawl-like position, you actually scooted forward on your own to get one of Tony's toy cars. Later, when I bounced you on a different developmental toy—a beach ball-like roll, you sat on it facing me and I held your feet flat on the floor to encourage a self-supporting weight-baring posture. You did bounce and straighten your legs enough to withstand some of your own weight. You were not actually standing up, but it was an improvement!

Have I mentioned teething lately? You have no teeth but have been gumming your mouth, chewing on diaper cloths, toys, and fingers since you were four months old. You are so funny! You suck on your lips in such a way that we have begun calling you "Granny without the dentures!" Wherever I go, people comment how cute you move your mouth—puckering, chewing, and sucking. You even play games with your tongue and have gotten to the point where you will smile, krinkle-up your nose, or laugh after you have done something particularly playful or funny with your little face!

⌒ JANUARY 4, 1982

Dear Jill,

Checkup time again. You weighed 15 pounds 12 ½ ounces and you are almost 29 inches long. Dr. Blum, however, thought that you looked duskier today and he increased your Lanoxin dose to .7. He saw more blue in your arms and legs and around your mouth. I commented that you wake up out of breath and appear to tire more easily. You are now only awake for two to three hours at a time. You have already had three naps today.

∽ JANUARY 5, 1982

Oh Jill,

We saw Dr. McCormick, the neurologist, today. I really do not care for this doctor. His manner is too casual and not caring enough. He speaks of seizures, spasms and cerebral palsy as if they were everyday terms to the average person. He could scare a parent to death without even trying! Although his observation of you was quite positive and encouraging, I still came a way from his office with a disgusted, negative feeling. Basically he said that *if* you suffered brain damage, you could fully recover, although the damage will always be there. But you can, and most likely will, live a full and normal life.

Cognitively you are ahead of your chronological age, which is very encouraging. It means that you should do quite well. God bless you, my little sweetheart. I swear that I will always do whatever is in my power to help you. I love you so much; it won't be hard to try my best to keep you challenged and developing every day.

Because I have noticed that you seem more tired lately, I have started keeping a log of your sleeping and eating patterns so that I can report to Dr. Katkov more accurately. You ate about twenty-seven ounces of formula today and slept a total of four hours during three naps. You were breathing hard during your "crawling exercises" and although you supported yourself on your stomach, you worked very hard to do so.

∽ JANUARY 6, 1982

Darling Jill,

You scooted backwards twice today! You rolled freely around on the floor, scooting backwards and lifting your head higher while lying on your tummy. You actually played with your feet when you were having a mini-bath in the kitchen sink, and then you tried to stand, but ended up "sputtering" instead!

∽ JANUARY 7, 1982

Jill,

You had occupational therapy today. You stood up twice while fully supporting your own weight. You didn't even notice the accomplishment because you were so busy looking at Mary Sivaroli's nametag! You have relaxed toward Mary. You let Mary hold you, feed, and play with you. Mary is so kind and loving. She is very good at her work and I know in my heart that you have benefited from Mary's expertise.

∽ JANUARY 10, 1982

Darling Jill,

I just finished an exercise session with you. Much to my delight you are holding yourself in a standing position with just my support at your hips or hands. Every day we practice exercises like sitting on top of the therapy roll for sitting balance and rolling over a smaller roll on the floor as a practice for crawling. We twist at your waist to reach a toy next to your side, sit without support while your feet are flat on the floor, pull up to a standing position, and play games like "pat-a-cake" to exercise your hands.

∽ JANUARY 11, 1982

Jill:

You have a cardiology appointment today. I must be fearful of losing you. I dreamed last night that we had another baby boy who weighed only three pounds and was delivered in the strangest way. In the dream you were still alive, but I can't help but think my dream was a way of validating that I need a baby to love and you are growing up so fast. It is scary to see you grow. At sixteen pounds, you are getting close to the prescribed twenty pounds necessary for your surgery.

My darling, I can't bear the thought that you might not make it through surgery. I know that I am being selfish in thinking that if you die that I will be lonely; I spend more time with you than anyone. Selfishly I feel as though I have the biggest emotional investment in your survival. Even so, when I see others interact with you my heart aches at the thought of you dying. When I see your dad hold you, I see how much he loves and treasures you. Ali and Tony adore you.

Last week I read a letter that Dr. Katkov wrote to your neurologist. In it he spoke of how serious your surgery will be and how complicated the procedure is to correct your heart defect. Just the way he wrote the letter snapped me back to reality. It was like a freezing splash of water on my face and my heart. The reality is you are *not* 100% fine and you may, in fact, die. When I think like that, I just want to stop time and love you just as you are now.

If only I could capture the feelings I have for you when I look at you, when I hold you, when I squeeze you and kiss you. I'd like to capture those feelings, save them and then release them when I get angry or sad. A mother's love for a baby can be so precious, so honest, so open, and so easy! If only we could always stay that loving, trusting, and easy-going with all our emotions.

Lately I have looked at the rest of my life and thought how complex relationships can be. It is then that I recognize how easy the love of my babies has been. It is so totally fulfilling. Coping with your heart surgery will be the hardest thing I will ever have to do. Overall I consider myself a lucky woman. I hope my good fortune holds out.

↩ JANUARY 16, 1982

Dear Jill,

Two days ago you began throwing up again for the first time in about three weeks. We went to therapy and you seemed almost lethargic, far less energetic than normal. You were continually crabby and by late afternoon you had a fever of 100°. I took you to see Dr. Blum who felt that although you looked pale, your color was better than the week before they raised the level of your Lanoxin medication. He thought you had a mild case of the stomach flu. I suppose he was right—you threw up three times and ate half your normal amount.

Yesterday you woke up *very* crabby. Ate and threw up your early morning breakfast and then slept on and off for the remainder of the morning. By nighttime there was a fever, but you appeared to be cramping and still somewhat sick.

Last week at your appointment with Dr. Katkov you were 16 pounds 1 ounce, at 29 inches long. Your age was nine months and one week. There were no exceptionally fast heartbeats (tachycardia) and the size of your heart and liver were the same as on your previous chest x-ray. You had an echocardiogram at Abbott Northwestern Hospital and fell asleep in my arms on the way there. I was so glad because you did not have to be sedated for the procedure.

Today we saw another doctor at Southdale Pediatrics. Your weight was down a bit, but we thought it was due to the stomach flu. You have been on diluted formula but you seem to be feeling better this afternoon. There is no fever and you have a good appetite, although you are still crabby and very tired. As I put you to bed tonight I noticed that you finally looked a little brighter. I am more confident that this minor flu episode is behind us. Things are looking up!

JANUARY 18, 1982

My dear Jill,

Yesterday you were better but you still woke up ravenous and crabby. You drank so much water and 7-Up! Gradually, throughout the day we increased the consistency of your formula so that by nighttime you ate almost a full eight ounces of a regular bottle with rice cereal and applesauce.

You slept in today until almost 7 A.M. We then spent a few hours at my mom's house because there was an open house at our house that is for sale and the realtor wanted us to leave. You got very tired and cranky so Ali and I rocked you to sleep in the trusty old infant seat. Last night I talked to Debby Cloud for one hour. We talked about you, babies in general, and what it must be like nursing so many sick babies, some of whom die.

⌒ JANUARY 20, 1982

Dear Jill,

It is nine o'clock in the evening and you were not better yesterday, so I took you in to see Dr. Blum. You have developed a cough and cold. By late yesterday you had a fever and the "sleeper crabbies." I sat with you on and off for four hours on Monday night to stop you from crying. By Tuesday, Dr. Blum determined that you had an ear infection and he started you on an antibiotic. You were supposed to be better by today, but...

Last night you cried until midnight. You finally fell asleep until about three o'clock in the morning. I then slept on the floor of your room and rocked you to sleep in the infant seat. I can't remember when you finally fell asleep, but I fell asleep next to you on the floor, holding your little chest and feeling your heart beat so very fast. Your breathing sounded awful and I tried to count the breaths.

⌒ JANUARY 21, 1982

Dear Jill,

Tonight I finally have my little "Jillsy" back! You are all smiles and giggles and laughs out loud! You just beamed whenever I came into the room. What a joy!

In the past five days I had truly forgotten how sweet your disposition is. Now that you are feeling better, your appetite is 100%. Your responsiveness and playfulness have also improved dramatically. Ali taught you to give her the "high five" and Tony just makes tons of noise and you smile like crazy! Your daddy taught you to put your "keppie" (head) down on his shoulder and I taught you to give me a kiss! These little things are so magical.

Yesterday I was talking about your eyes to Angie, our wonderful cleaning lady and friend, who has loved you from the very first day she saw you at six days old. Anyway, Angie used to say that your eyes told her when you are happy. She said they light up when you smile. Well, yesterday, I told Angie that many times I look into your eyes and you just look back at me with a look of "I KNOW." The deep perceptions I see in your eyes tell me that you know the future. Sometimes I believe that you can see inside my soul. Sometimes, I will talk to you about dying, either silently or out loud, and those little eyes just look at me as if they know all of the answers. If only they could say, "Mommy, everything is going to be all right!"

When I get worried about your upcoming surgery, I just concentrate on the cute things you do. In combination, they make me laugh and appreciate your genuine infant antics! Sometimes you just sit on the kitchen counter watching us cook or work in the kitchen. When Ali or Tony are eating, you lean far forward to see around the TV and get a really good look at what they are doing at the kitchen table. When I put your snowsuit on, you chew on the hood string, so I always have to tie it with it going through your mouth!

We have had an extremely cold winter with lots of snow. Yesterday I put your snowsuit on, and then left you sitting in your infant seat in the kitchen while I went to warm up the car in the garage. When I came back, there you were, this little bundled baby, looking like a lost soul. But as soon as you saw me, you beamed with recognition and anticipation.

You have also done a really good job learning the word "NO." Whenever I say "No" or "Mommy says no" your face breaks out into a scrunched-up cry. You can definitely sense when someone isn't happy. Your devastation expression happens even when I whisper the word "No." I have learned to very gently reprimand you and only when it is absolutely necessary. Believe me, I rarely say anything that will make that precious face scrunch up and cry.

⌒ JANUARY 24, 1982

Good morning, Jill,

It is early Sunday morning and you and I are snuggled in my big bed. You just finished the last of a bottle while I had my first cup of coffee. As I write in this diary, you are playing with your basket of rattles and toys. This morning, your daddy tried to surprise me by getting you up, changing your diaper and feeding you while I slept. All went well until you decided that he wasn't moving fast enough with the bottle and you screamed at the top of your lungs until I came downstairs. Oh, well, at least he tried. Actually, you seem a little crabbier today anyway. Your cold is still there. Your nose is running and your cough seems thick and heavy. I will probably take you to the doctor tomorrow if the cough is not better.

This 1982 winter is by far the worst Minnesota winter that I can remember. This week alone, we have had two of the worst blizzards in history. On Wednesday we had seventeen inches of snow and then on Friday we had eighteen more. The snow is unbelievably high, and because of the high winds and bad roads, the city is closed up. Ali came home from school and your dad's office closed early. All activities for the weekend have been canceled.

Last night, you sat in your favorite "Daddy snuggle spot" while we all watched TV. You sort of sit on his lap and a little off to the side of him in his favorite leather chair. And to keep you happy, he lets you play with the remote control to the TV. You are so cute sitting there. You put your "keppie" on his shoulder, you hit his chest with your hand in your favorite "bam-bam" game, and every once in a while you changed the TV channel by pressing the remote control!

Ah, the big news of the day: Your first tooth has arrived! It just popped through the gum! Your new word is "Hi" and you mimic me whenever I say it. Your other favorite sound is "b-b-b" for "ba-ba-bottle." Developmentally, we were at a standstill the last week and a half because you were sick. We have not done any exercises or play therapy since January 14, and you haven't attempted any crawling, standing, or further exploring on your own. You still talk a great deal and try to play pat-a-cake, but you have mastered the game "How big is Jill?" by putting your hands way up in the air. Your language consists of mostly "Da-Da" (for daddy *and* mommy!), "Ga-Ga" (for good girl), "Cawl" (for cold *and* duck), and sometimes you just jabber with sounds like "ya-ya-ya" and "rah-rah-rah." All that for a little girl who is not quite ten months old!

⌒ JANUARY 27, 1982

My darling Jill,

You have been adorable today. 100% back to normal! You are happy, smiley, and talkative. You have had energy all day and your new little tooth clinks against a spoon. The big news came two nights ago when Ali baby-sat with you while daddy and I ate dinner. She said that you tried to pull yourself up on a table. Sure enough, when I placed you next to the coffeetable you stood holding on for a few seconds! You are pulling yourself to a stand better each day when you are in your playpen or holding onto my hands. Today you actually said "car" while you were playing with one of Tony's toy cars and you are becoming more and more demanding with the "b-b-b" when you want your bottle!

Angie baby-sat for you today while she was at our house. You recognize her now and seem to just love her! You chatted and smiled all morning for her and you even kept looking for Angie when she left for the day.

◌ THURSDAY, JANUARY 28, 1982

My darling Jill,

It is 10 P.M. and you are sound asleep. Today at OT therapy with Mary Sivaroli you had one of the best sessions ever. You did not cry at all. You stood up several times for Mary and you even appeared to understand the word "Up" when Mary said it by offering her hands to you.

You did not attempt to crawl but you let Mary work with you in several positions including kneeling, laying on your tummy, scooting forward, and going from sitting to stomach. You even inched forward on all fours with much support from Mary. Every little tiny motion means so much! Today you seemed more thoughtful and concerned about each thing that you did. You looked at Mary and at each new toy carefully and all in all you responded absolutely adorably today. My dear, you even seemed terribly proud of yourself whenever you accomplished something that elicited a "good girl" from Mary or me. What is even funnier is that if you did something that you felt deserved a "good girl" you looked at us as if to say, "Well?" You kissed Mary goodbye and seemed not to want to leave her today.

After therapy we went to see Dr. Chisholm. He felt it was very good that your hand wound was still spitting out pieces of calcium but it looked improved to him. He said the scar did not seem as deep or the skin as tough as before. I have not seen any difference, although it does turn less white when I bend your hand downward during hand exercises. The size of your fingers is a little bit better (less swollen) and the color of your left hand is getting closer to normal. There is one little blood spot where I expect a piece of calcium to pop out once the skin breaks. We will have to wait and see. Getting rid of calcium is a good thing. It means the hand is becoming more flexible and softening from the burn wound.

You still cry easily when I do your hand therapy. I still do it at least once every day and when things are not that hectic, I try to do it twice.

You love to hear your new tooth clink against a spoon. You played with your daddy tonight and even said "Da-dee" several times quite clearly. I thought I heard you say "Jill" in therapy today and so did Mary. I also imagined (wishful thinking on my part) that you said "ma." But it didn't happen. I wonder if it ever will?

⌒ FRIDAY, JANUARY 29, 1982

Good morning, Jill:

Today is picture day! The photographer is coming to the house late morning right after your nap. We are also going to see Dr. Blum for a check up to see if your ear infection is cleared up.

It is now evening and you are asleep. You looked absolutely precious for your picture today. I couldn't have asked for more—every pose seemed to be perfect. Oh, I do hope they turn out! The photographer took twelve pictures, ten regular ones and two close-ups. In my heart, I know the close-up pictures will be very special. I saw the twinkle in your eye and the softness of your cheek, just as the camera clicked to capture your precious image.

Today, you weighed 15 pounds 14 ounces at the doctor's office and you were 29 ¼ inches long. Your ear infection is all gone and you are just a few days away from ten months old.

∽ TUESDAY, FEBRUARY 2, 1982

My darling Jill,

YOU DID IT! Finally, you did it. Tonight you said "Ma." During the last few days you have had a variety of sounds in your play talking and I thought I heard "ma" on a few other occasions. But tonight I know I heard it for sure.

Last night you stayed in a four-point crawling position during exercise therapy with me. I had to help you reach for a toy, but it was the first time you did not flop onto your tummy and collapse. You actually stayed in the kneeling position for a few moments.

You love to stand up. You can pull yourself up too. You get really excited to see us in the morning when we come into your room and get you from your crib. How do I know you are excited? Well, you just wiggle and kick your legs straight up and down over and over again! Then you will give me a kiss good morning. You love to see Ali and Tony in the morning and since your dad is usually at the office by the time you wake up, you don't get excited to see him until night.

You have become quite demanding and very impatient about getting your bottle. When you want it, you want it! You start looking for it when you get hungry and keep saying "b-b-b" over and over until it appears!

It is hard to believe that you will be ten months old tomorrow. It is also so hard to believe that you, the little joy of my life, who seems so happy and easy to care for, have had so much pain and discomfort in your life. The problems like all the vomiting and colic episodes seem so long ago. Sometimes I feel like I just can't get enough of you. I can't kiss you enough, touch, hold, or squeeze you enough, or even just love you enough. But other times, it is just enough to sit and watch you. Just looking at you, my precious, fragile, little girl is enough. I love you with all my heart and soul.

∽ WEDNESDAY, FEBRUARY 3, 1982

Jillsy, you are ten months old today and your second tooth has arrived!

∽ SUNDAY, FEBRUARY 7, 1982

Dear Jill,

It is early morning. You just cried out in your sleep and woke me up. This is the third night in a row that you have been restless. I don't understand it because yesterday your day was quite good. You, Ali, and Tony went over to Grandma Phyl's for five hours where you talked, played, and slept in your infant seat. Grandma told me that you said the sound "ma-ma-ma" over and over all day. Just a few days ago, on Thursday, you had OT with Mary again. You worked very hard. Mary worked with you on the crawling position, scooting forward, kneeling, and standing. You huffed and puffed and because of your heavy breathing we felt you were working very hard. You put your head down several times, but didn't seem sleepy. I sort of thought you were just playing with us and wanted us to see how hard you were working! What was interesting was that you definitely prefer to move out of a sitting position, into a crawling stance from one side only. You turn toward the right side and you will propel yourself completely around in a circle to obtain the correct position to fall forward out of sitting.

Tonight I wanted to practice your exercises more because I feel that I have been somewhat lax with you. We are now in the process of moving to our new house and so I have been very busy with other things. In my heart I feel that if I were to try and spend just a smidge more time with you perhaps you would finally achieve the appropriate movements toward crawling. You actually rocked on your hands and knees today alone without support and that in itself was a big step! You really did well supporting yourself on hands and knees while reaching for a toy.

Also today, you played pat-a-cake by putting your left hand (the one with the burn) over the right for the first time! Wonderful to see that growth!

TUESDAY, FEBRUARY 9, 1982

My dear little one:

Well, you haven't said "Ma" since Sunday! But guess what? You just now went from a sitting to a crawling position almost completely unsupported on your hands and knees. You have definitely improved this week in all your attempts to crawl. You stand longer and stronger now. And yes, you are finally "rocking" on all fours!

Yesterday you ate your first Oreo cookie. It is the only solid food that you love! I cut your hair a smidge tonight because there were a few wispy long ends. And of course, as always, when your daddy came through the door after work, you got so excited to see him. You even say "Dada" to him as soon as he comes into sight. Your favorite game to play now, with him, is what he calls "the raspberries." It is a game he taught you. You make lots of bubbles and a bubbly sound with your lips. As soon as you see him now, you do the raspberries! So cute!

FRIDAY NIGHT, FEBRUARY 12, 1982

Dear Jill,

A chapter in our lives is ending. In just four nights we are moving to the new house. Tomorrow is the box moving day and Sunday is "getting organized" day and then Monday is packing, with the move happening on Tuesday. As we get ready to move, I feel sad. It is about you growing older more than about leaving this house.

You are ten-and-a-half months old. Babyhood and infancy seem like they are coming to a close. I love Ali and Tony very much, but as children grow, the innocent, open, honest love melts away as a more mature complex relationship takes its place. But with you, it feels different.

Tonight you were absolutely precious and so excited to be with us. First of all, you started talking as soon as your dad came through the door. You are really learning about what we say and do. You know to play the raspberries game with him and you know to try and bounce up and down when I sing your favorite game song "Pop goes the Weasel." You even tried to put your sock back on your toes when I took it off yesterday. It is so fun to interact with you—every little movement and action means so much.

When you get excited, your face just breaks out in biggest smile. A smile that includes closed eyes, huge cheeks, and a little red nose! You wiggle your whole body when you think someone is going to pick you up. You get excited for Ali and Tony and you are content to play in the same room with them for almost an hour.

The only thing that you didn't want to do was go to sleep tonight. You, my little angel, are still moaning in your crib right now.

⌾ SATURDAY, FEBRUARY 13, 1982

My little Jill,

It is 3:00 in the morning and I just can't sleep. I have peeked at you, Ali, and Tony. I have read and written a list of things to do. What I would love to do is just snuggle in bed with you next to me. You always look so warm and snuggly, and yet you never fall sleep in my arms in my bed.

Have I told you that you no longer stick out your fabulous lower lip when you get angry or are pouting? Somewhere in the last two to three weeks you decided to crinkle up your nose and shut your eyes when you get upset. It is so cute, but not as cute as the pouting lower lip. You pull yourself up on furniture now. You don't get more than your little tushy off the ground, but you try nonetheless. You have also been trying to drink water out of a cup. Most of it spills but you sure love trying. Well, I best try to get some sleep. Tomorrow is going to be another busy day.

⌒ MONDAY EVENING, FEBRUARY 15, 1982

Dear Jill:

All three of you children spent yesterday at Grandma Phyl's house in preparation for the move tomorrow. You were awake almost the whole day because I forgot to bring over your infant seat, but you finally fell asleep with Grandma rocking you. Grandma said that you were an angel all day.

Today you have been good as well. You drank your bottle, napped and watched the packers. Late in the day, you, Ali, and I went over to the new house and you played on the floor of Ali's new room while I worked putting things away. We had a fast-food dinner from Arby's (you had formula) and then you were in bed by seven o'clock.

You are asleep now and looking so precious and peaceful. Jill, you represent a very important part of our move to the big, new house. It is a good move because it brings excitement and a new energy to a household that has been totally concentrating only on you. And yet, I can only hope that all will be okay as we move into the future.

I would feel an overwhelming loneliness if I were to be alone in that big house without you, Jill. The move means we are moving forward and yet it brings us closer to your surgery. I can only face tomorrow and each new day with the hope of getting the most out of life. I can only think about living each day to the fullest and loving all my children deeply and with no regrets. Here's to the future of health, happiness, love, and miracles— especially for you, my precious little one…Jill Elizabeth Davis.

✪ THURSDAY, FEBRUARY 18, 1982

My dear Jill:

We went to therapy today for the first time in two weeks. It was a fabulous session. We used the observation/play room instead of the normal outpatient examining room for the first time. You had twice as much room to move around and, hence, were twice as active! You did fantastically. You almost crawled. It was the closest you ever came to crawling. When I put you on all fours, you rocked back and forth until you took two "steps" with your hands and, although your knees stayed stationary, you looked a lot like crawling! You loved playing with all the new toys. You don't cry at all any more during OT and you actually play with Mary. Your facial expressions are incredible. You are making so much progress as you work on crawling, kneeling, pulling up to a stand, and going from a sitting position to a crawling motion.

✪ SATURDAY, FEBRUARY 20, 1982

Dear Jill,

I can hardly believe that four days have passed since moving into our new house on Lake of the Isles. It was an exhilarating and very busy day. The newness of all the rooms and wide-open spacious floor plan made the work of putting things away seem like fun. The Italian Renaissance house is approximately 100 years old, situated in a prestigious neighborhood and very large—8,000 square feet. The architecture presents a majestic appearance. It has five bedrooms, maids' quarters, and eight bathrooms. The master bedroom has a fireplace, two dressing rooms, a double-sized bathroom, and a complete sitting area for two chairs, a loveseat, and a television. Ali has her own bedroom and bath, while you and Tony have adjoining bedrooms connected by your bathroom. There's also guest suite (the size of most master bedrooms), a tiny office hideaway for me to use as my calligraphy studio, and a clothes chute that drops the dirty laundry down two flights into a giant laundry cage (a great hiding place for kids who don't mind the smell).

The main floor has an enormous living room with a marble fireplace, super-high ceilings, an informal sunroom (a cozy sort of family room with lots of windows), and a very large dining room that comfortably seats twelve to twenty people. One of my favorite rooms is the mahogany library with gorgeous bookshelves and a small cornerstone fireplace. There are matching his-and-her guest bathrooms on either side of the front door, and at one time, I imagine they were privileged to have been occupied by many a "who's who" in Minneapolis during formal dinner parties.

We remodeled the kitchen and back hall suite of rooms prior to moving in. We have the most deluxe kitchen design I have ever experienced, a beautiful breakfast room/dining area with many cupboards and a full wet bar. Off to the side of the kitchen is the children's playroom with many toy cupboards for all of your games and playthings, a window seat, and my desk and writing area. The basement has both an informal and formal side to it with matching staircases—the informal one leading to the laundry room, and the formal circular staircase making its way down to a lower level office and a historic large ballroom. The formal front entryway into the house has marble floors, a two-level ceiling, and a circular staircase and railing, all of which give the circular entry room a grand, rotundalike effect.

Moving day began with you getting up at 7 A.M., having a bottle, and getting all ready to move to your new house. I, of course, was up much earlier, so very excited to begin the final phase of our moving adventure. You and I left to go over to the new house right after the movers arrived. Our goal was to unpack food and kitchen items while the movers loaded furniture onto the truck at the old house.

You played in your playpen while I put food away in the kitchen. You wouldn't take a nap, so I made you a bottle in the new microwave. Oops! It got too hot. I tried to give you a nap in the buggy but you refused. You finally fell asleep, late morning, just as the movers arrived with furniture. You slept until lunch and then we played in our new living room on the rug while the movers took their lunch break.

During the afternoon after your next bottle, you followed me around and played on the floor of each of the children's rooms while I made their beds. I put your playpen in the corner of our sunroom; you love to play in it and peek at whoever is in the room or walking by. You seemed comfortable playing on the floor in all rooms of the house provided there were toys or things to touch nearby.

As the movers put the last piece of furniture in your room, you were ready for your afternoon nap. Miss Jill, you were the first person totally unpacked in the new Davis Residence on the Lake Parkway. Your clothes were the first to be placed in the closets, your toys, bottles, food, and necessities were the first to be unpacked and used. You must have been wonderfully busy and excited during the day, because for your first night in the new house you slept almost thirteen hours!

⚭ FEBRUARY 24, 1982

Dearest Jill,

Yesterday was my thirtieth birthday. But unfortunately, on Monday morning, you got sick. You woke up with a temperature of almost 101° and by late morning it was 102°. I immediately took you to the doctor where everything checked out okay. As a precaution, you were put on Erythromycin. Because fevers are more serious with heart babies, I get more scared than I would otherwise when you are sick. Your temperature stayed high until Tuesday morning and then you seemed to do okay.

My birthday has always been a special day. I had always wanted three children by the time I was thirty. It felt like I had a lot to celebrate. Jillsy, you were a doll all day. We had a big birthday party last night and you played in your playpen for a while during dinner. I held you during the birthday cake dessert, gave you a bottle, and you fell asleep around eight o'clock.

There was a mystical feeling in my heart as I blew out the candles. At thirty years old, I felt there was a life passage hinged on this day. However, your health and survival are integral to my birthday vision for my future.

∽ FEBRUARY 25, 1982

Darling Jill:

Today you had therapy with Mary again. And it was another super day. Again, you just almost crawled. You scoot with your knees but move your hands forward one at a time. Mary had a new toy that you loved. It was a pull-string, talking toy. It was fun to watch you be so curious and inquisitive with something new. Mary also used two coins that she had you place in a drawer. It was wonderful to see you grasp the concept of "putting in." At home you put plastic toy shapes into their respective boxes and you even try to put the lids on the toy containers. But my favorite activity is when you try what I call "press and stick" with things like your socks. You pick up a sock that falls off and put it on your foot hoping it will stick back on! The coolest thing is that you hold your own bottle now. You drink almost thirty-two ounces daily. We keep hoping that you gain weight and become stronger for your anticipated surgery.

While I would love to write more, I have a terrible cold and am tired now. I best go to sleep and get my energy for taking care of you and the new big house. I hope you don't get my cold, little one.

↷ MONDAY, MARCH 1, 1982

Oh Jill,

You caught my cold. You are extra cranky, crying a great deal today. Your nose is bright red. We saw Dr. Blum. He diagnosed your bright red nose as impetigo and now you are back on Erythromycin. He also took cultures and I am supposed to call tomorrow for the results. Ah, tomorrow—Jill, you have another heart catheterization scheduled. Another scary time.

↷ TUESDAY, MARCH 2, 1982

Dearest Jill,

I am sitting on the floor of the Abbott Northwestern Hospital hallway outside the surgical waiting room. Your heart cath started a few minutes ago. It has been a very emotional morning and a very scary look into the future. I woke you up at 6:30 this morning, changed your diaper, and put you into a snowsuit. We kissed Ali and your dad good-bye (Tony was still sleeping) and drove to Children's Hospital. We got here just before 7 A.M.—actually ahead of the admitting department. After you were checked in, I put you in a hospital gown; they took your temperature and a urine sample.

Then we went up to the lab for your blood work. They had to prick your finger three times and press hard to squeeze out enough blood to fill three vials. It was terrible for you and painful for me to watch. You screamed and pushed the lab tech's hand away. You arched your back and cried so hard that it just made me sick. Once the blood work episode was over, you got to have a sponge bath to cleanse you for the surgical procedure. Now that was fun! You had toys and a brush to play with, so you played "splash-splash" and got water all over the tub, the counter, and the floor! Finally you turned blue and I got you out and into a clean diaper and hospital pajama. You then got wrapped in a warm blanket that my grandmother, Ma, knit for you and you snuggled against me for warmth. The only good time up to that point was when everyone left us alone and you talked and played in the tub, oblivious to the rest of the hospital setting.

At 8:30 A.M., you were sitting on my lap when your favorite nurse, Deb, came into the Short Stay Unit (SSU) to see you. You just stared at Deb. Then your dad walked in. When you saw your daddy, you smiled and talked and said Dada. You were so happy to see him. There were tears in his eyes. I don't really know how much he admits this to anyone, but he loves you so. I never saw him hurt so much for anyone as he does at the thought of losing you.

Anyway, you smiled and played with your dad, Deb, and Mary Sivaroli, who also came down to the SSU to say hi before the heart cath procedure. The time went by quickly. You only asked for your bottle three times and didn't really seem to miss it that much when we couldn't give you anything to eat or drink. You were too busy looking around, watching and listening to every single sound and movement in the hospital unit. You didn't trust anyone and mostly just snuggled up against me while you played little games with your dad.

At nine o'clock you got a shot with three kinds of sedation. You and I both cried. You cried because the needle in your leg hurt and I cried because of the overwhelming fear that you will run into trouble and not wake up. You snuggled closer and closer to me as we walked over to the Abbott Northwestern cath lab. Finally, halfway there your head began to bob and I shifted positions and cradled you in my arms. You kept opening your eyes for one last look and then got a helpless, limp, and sickly look about you. I kept feeling sick inside—it was so different from holding you when you are asleep.

It is overwhelming to think that my spunky, bright, beautiful little Jillsy-bean could go to sleep for an operation that she might never come out of. Anyway, this diary helps fill the time. It is ten o'clock in the morning and we have about two more hours. "Do a good job, little Jill." We love you and want you back.

⌒ THURSDAY, MARCH 4, 1982

Dearest Jill,

It has now been two days since your heart catheterization. All went well. Our little Jillsy is almost back to normal. You did very well; had no major problems and came home with us Tuesday night. You have slowly gotten back into your daily routine. But so much happened during the cath. They had trouble getting the catheters into your veins. At about 11:45 A.M. they came out to say that they had one line in; one line had to be put in by making an incision and they had not explored all parts of the heart yet because it was so hard. They thought you might be done by 12:30 P.M.

Sure enough, at 12:45 P.M., Dr. Katkov came out to say that you came through it okay with no sustained abnormal heart rhythms. I had forgotten about the chance of heart arrhythmias and irregular beating. The doctors said that your pulmonary band was doing its job, but that it was so tight that it took five catheter sizes to get one small enough to fit through it. The doctors think that they got good pictures of the inside of your heart, and if they can review them carefully, they should be able to tell us more in a week or two.

There was some mix-up with the nurse who was releasing you, so unfortunately, we didn't get to see you until early afternoon. You were already semi-awake and drinking your second bottle of sugar water. You stared at us with very sleepy eyes, said a little "dada," and finally, a bit later, you drifted into a sound sleep. They had given you a shot of Demerol, Phenergon, and Thorazine and it really knocked you out.

Our favorite nurses from LSU came over to the Short Stay Unit to see you. Deb Cloud held you on her lap until almost four o'clock in the afternoon. Gloria Nelson, the head of the LSU, and Paula and Janet, two other favorite nurses, came to see you too. You had to keep your right leg straight for two hours after the catheterization so that there was no bleeding from the puncture site, plus you had seven stitches on the left side of your groin. That side was also where you had your shot and it's been very sensitive. You haven't used your leg normally since the heart cath.

Anyway, when I got you home at 5:30 P.M., you were still kind of staring into space. I tenderly held you in the silence of your room and then put you to bed, but woke you up at 8:30 P.M. for a bottle of diluted formula and your heart medicine, Lanoxin.

It was actually a quiet night. I fell asleep just after you went to bed and slept restlessly all night. Your dad put the intercom next to our bed but you hardly made any noises until early the next morning. I fed you again and checked your diaper. Your right catheter opening had been bleeding. You went back to sleep early and were up again a few hours later. Your lethargy bothered me and you hadn't moved much since the catheterization, plus you hadn't given us any regular "Jillsy" smiles, so I took you to see Dr. Katkov later that morning. He felt that everything seemed to be okay, so I brought you home in time for a late morning nap. When you woke up, your eyes had a sparkle and your smile had returned. You played on the floor and I began to feel better too. When I changed your diaper, the area was still very sensitive. So I have been giving you Baby Tylenol drops every four hours.

My little darling, you finally felt well enough to smile, and when your dad came home you gave him your usual Jillsy-bean smile with a cheerful sounding "Da-dee." As before, you giggled and got so excited to see him. You only want me to hold you, but you really want him to play with you! Today, however, when you played on the floor, you kept your left leg straight when trying to crawl. You cried again tonight when I put you to bed, but you finally fell asleep and are peacefully slumbering now.

∽ MONDAY, MARCH 8, 1982

Dear Jill:

Last night you almost crawled! You went from a sitting position to all fours, moved your hands forward, moved one knee forward, then you lay down, got back up onto all fours, and lastly pushed yourself up into a sitting position.

My little munchkin, you can also figure out how to get your hand bandage off without first taking off the adhesive tape! You take it off every single day at least once. Yesterday we took a buggy ride around the lake. It was quite cold so you had a snowsuit, mittens, scarf, and blanket with you. You sat up in the buggy and had a ball! The wind blew against you and you had sparkles on your cheeks with a red and purple glow.

Your dad is out of town tonight. You and he had a little bit of a discipline lesson last Saturday night. It appears that you knowingly dropped all of your toys on the floor while he was watching you (I was upstairs taking a bath). Evidently, every time you dropped something, he would say "NO" and then you would look right at him before doing it again. The episode ended with a stern "daddy reprimand" and a ton of Jillsy tears.

You and I saw Dr. Owen at Sister Kenney Institute today. He said that you don't need to wear your arm brace for a while. Your hand flexion is forty-five degrees and your extension is eighty degrees. He suggested that you continue OT one time per week. He said that your crawling helps to break up the scar tissue in your hand, and it helps loosen the calcium to allow more flexion in your wrist. He was pleased to see that you played pat-a-cake today by clapping both hands openly in front. That is progress!

Now how could I forget the big news? Twice today, you called "ma" when I was not in the room. You were in your crib one time, and on the floor of my room the other, when I heard something that sounded a lot like "M-m-ma." When I came into the room super excited, you wouldn't say it again. So, it just might have been my imagination that my little Jillsy-bean said "Ma." In any case, it took my breath away to believe it really happened.

MONDAY EVENING, MARCH 15, 1982

My little Jill:

I just put you to bed for the night. Your lips were very blue and I am concerned about you. You seemed exceptionally tired tonight so I guess the extra blue could be a result of your being overtired. Today was not one of your best days. It started when Tony woke you up too early and your stuffy nose made you throw up even before breakfast. The day continued with several more episodes of throwing up and a few sessions of the crabbies. Hopefully tomorrow will be a better day. Sleep well, little one.

MARCH 17, 1982

Dearest Jill,

It is an hour past your bedtime and I can hardly stand to put you to bed. You are so cute, so precious, and you have so many mannerisms and expressions that I just love. Try as I might to write everything down, I am afraid that I won't capture every last detail of your life to remember about you.

Today I got a preliminary report from one of your doctors that you may be having heart surgery this summer. It sounded easy to handle until I realized this summer was only three months away. At that moment, my heart sank.

To think we might have you in our lives for only three more months seems overwhelmingly unbearable. I can't imagine the devastation any of us would feel at losing you.

∽ MARCH 19, 1982

Darling Jill:

Is it possible for the love of a child to grow stronger and more intense each day? Sometimes there are moments when I feel I could burst with how much I love you and then I feel as if there is this strong need to capture every moment with you and to gather every breath of life from you. I never thought the time before surgery would be this hard. I often feel flippant about the fact that your surgery is so dangerous and yet so necessary.

As I have thought before, my only mistake would be in thinking I am the only one suffering with this anticipation. Yesterday your dad admitted to me, for the very first time in our married life, that he can't handle his own pain and mine as well. Earlier this week we started talking about your surgery and he became angry with me about it. I had cried because I realized that I might only have a few months left with you. Fear dripped from my soul with every tear. Your dad and I ended up fighting the whole night.

The next morning I realized we just wouldn't survive doing it this way—with him angry and me depressed. If you die, we would probably separate, never able to console each other and then what kind of life would there be? We decided that we each must handle our own grief and in turn we have to be strong together. It really does tear me up inside to see him look at you. There is such adoring love in his eyes and I know he feels as I do inside. What is so unreal is that your dad just isn't the "old soft touch" kind of person. So this is so out of character for him.

Ali and Tony, on the other hand, are terribly involved with you. Lately, Ali hasn't been as verbal as Tony, but she carries her emotions differently. Just the other day Tony started talking about dying and then the next day he told me "Jill has been good to us, so let's be good to her and we'll pick up her toys whenever she drops them, okay?" And then he added, "Mom, don't say 'No' to Jill anymore." Who knows what he is feeling? But it must be very perceptive and intuitive.

I must remember that this journal is meant to be a wonderful remembrance of you and all the cute things you do. I can't get too melancholy or fearful of that which may never happen. Instead, I could fill the pages with so many cute "Jillsy" things. My favorite, and yours, of course, is "Pop" or "Pop goes the weasel." The toy Jack-in-the-box and the song "Pop-goes-the-weasel" are both your favorites. Anywhere, anytime, you bounce up and down to play "pop" and you know the song and love to hear it. You laugh out loud at the "Pop" part of the song and you are so cute, waiting in anticipation of that moment. You love being tossed up in the air or tickled, or just squeezed in enjoyment and love.

Oh, my goodness, there are so many cute things you do. I can always squeeze a smile out of you. I say "squeeze" or give you a tight little hug and out comes the brightest little smile. You are so cute with your little kisses and your "Jillsy" snuggles are sooooo good!

I love to rock with you in the rocking chair in your room. It can be in the middle of the day or in the darkness of the night and you will snuggle in close to me while we are rocking. You often lift your little head to look at me while we are rocking. In those moments, I just immerse myself in your eyes.

⌒ SATURDAY MARCH 20, 1982

Good morning Jill:

I woke up to find you sitting up in your crib, talking away and playing by yourself. I fed you a small bottle, changed you, and then we snuggled a bit. But you would not go back to sleep. When your dad woke up, he came in and told you to be quiet. Your face scrunched up, your nose and cheeks turned red, and you started to cry. Well, that won us over immediately! We then pulled you into bed with us where you seemed really happy. You snuggled in next to me and we fell asleep until your dad brought me a cup of coffee. You popped your head up the minute he entered the room. You then made a little "kiss" sound with your mouth puckered up. I melted! It was a lovely way to start the day.

⌒ TUESDAY, MARCH 23, 1982

Oh Jill,

Yesterday was a terrible day—one of the worst days that I can remember lately. It started when you woke up screaming at four o'clock in the morning. You needed to be comforted and fed. You seemed to want to play and we did so. But later you threw up your whole breakfast and messed up all of your clothes.

Later, when I was giving you a second breakfast, you fell out of your highchair in a "split second" moment of carelessness on my part. You then threw up again. I felt awful. I had been wiping your face and hands, and just as I took the highchair tray off and put it on the counter, you leaned forward before I was ready to catch you—and you fell to the floor. I think that I was sicker than you were about the whole thing. But later that day, when you threw up again I began to worry that something was seriously wrong.

In the afternoon I took you to see Dr. Katkov. He said that you were fine from the morning fall. You had one last suture removed from your catheter stitches. While I was there, I tried to talk to him about your upcoming surgery and even went so far as to pin him down to suggest a date that it would take place.

For the first time ever, his frank and honest style made me depressed and scared. He told me that "we need to help her— she is getting bluer because the pulmonary band is getting too tight." He said that he and Dr. Helseth, the thoracic surgeon, needed to decide whether to do a temporary procedure or whether to attempt your open-heart corrective surgery. The temporary procedure would be to put a shunt in to get more blood to your lungs. It would be a "closed-heart" procedure and it would buy us more time until you were bigger and could tolerate the open-heart surgery. Dr. K said that he was going to present your case to another group of doctors early Thursday morning after which he would talk to us.

The doctors' roundtable discussion was a standard procedure in complex cases and it gave the primary doctor every opportunity to determine alternatives and the best course of action. The doctors' summit should be a sense of comfort for me, but the entire conversation filled me with dread and depressed my own heart in anticipation of what lies ahead.

After you and I got home from our visit to Dr. Katkov, you took a nap, played, and ate until I put you to bed at 8:30 P.M. You screamed for a half-hour at which point you threw up for the fourth time that day. I finally got you to quiet down and go to sleep about an hour later. Needless to say, I tossed and turned all night and dreamed about how blue you are becoming. Ever since your heart cath indicated that you need your surgery soon, I am growing increasingly afraid and depressed. My heart wants to hug you and my mind wants to scream out my fear.

↺ SUNDAY NIGHT, MARCH 28, 1982

My dear Jillsy-bean:

It is hard to believe that one year ago tonight I sat writing in a diary about the expected birth of a baby who would enter my life and change it drastically just by being born. And now, one year later, I write in the same baby's diary, only this time, I write of not an exciting forthcoming event, but of a dreaded, frightening future date when I won't be getting a *new* baby but when I might possibly be losing the baby that I have grown to love with all my heart.

So many thoughts are dancing around in my head. Just a few minutes ago, I put you, my precious little Jillsy, in your bed for the night. I wanted desperately to write of your soft, plump little cheeks, your playful smile, and your sweet, yet piercing eyes that seem to understand much more than a child your age should be able to.

Tonight, I really wanted to write about your hugs and snuggles and when your whole body crawls up to me to kiss me with sweet innocence. But I feel compelled to write a complete entry about our meeting with Dr. Katkov last Thursday morning. It has been four days now, and each day I have wanted desperately to be alone to fill these pages with my thoughts and feelings—and yet, what could I say that I have not said before about the horrible anticipation of your surgery?

Dr. Katkov surprised me, but not your dad, when he recommended that you have your open-heart surgery in the next thirty to sixty days, by the end of May for sure. So in a decisive, heart-aching moment we scheduled your surgery to take place at Children's Health Center on Wednesday, May 19, 1982. We will probably confirm the date when we sit down with Dr. K, Dr. Blum and, hopefully, Dr. Helseth, the surgeon.

In the meantime, it is our understanding that Dr. Helseth has never actually done a "double outlet transposition" corrective surgery exactly like this before. The difference is in the exact location of your ventricle septal defect (the hole in your heart). Your defect apparently lies right below the pulmonary artery making the rerouting of your red and blue blood just that much more difficult. Anyway, Dr. K suggests that there is really only one other heart surgeon in the world who might do better for you. His name is Dr. Castenada from Boston Children's Hospital. Dr. Helseth actually trained with the Boston doctor. Evidently, Dr. K will be talking with Dr. Castenada in the next two weeks after he sends him the catheterization films to review. The question they need to determine is whether your chance for survival will be increased if Dr. Castenada does the surgery

instead of Dr. Helseth. The other reason for their phone conference will be to determine whether Dr. Castenada is in agreement
with what needs to be done and when.

Believe me, I have thought about all the choices over and over.
In some ways, Boston would be harder on you and us, but if
your chance for survival greatly increases by going there, then we
must come to a decision based on the information we receive by
our doctors here. We will have more information soon, after
their phone conference on April 8.

Last Thursday morning, our meeting with Dr. K was very
frightening for me for two reasons: First, the discussion of procedures, with medical terminology relating to your heart, has
become so much a part of my thinking that it scares me when I
suddenly realize that I am talking about my sweet precious baby.
I forget that your heart is so terribly mixed up and I don't even
think about the fact that someone is going to cut you open, stop
your heart, and try to fix it. The whole idea that my little baby
will be sick before she is better makes me sad and scared. Oh,
God, the respirator, the heart monitors, the lung therapy, the
awful big scar, the tubes, the IVs—oh, YICH. Go away.

The second scary realization of Thursday's meeting was the
hardest one to face: the fact that we now finally have a time limit
on our love for you, Jill. We may have less than two months to
love you and have you in our lives. I absolutely can't imagine life
without you. You are woven into our thoughts, our daily rou-
tines, and our hearts.

All day Thursday I felt sick inside—empty and alone. I ran
errands and left you at home with Angie, who loves to care for
you by holding you in her arms. In my heartsick state of mind,
I wandered into a porcelain shop that sold little figurines like the
ones I had been collecting for ten years. I suddenly found a
Royal Copenhagen statue of a little girl in a blue sweater sitting
down with her arms stretched upwards. She appeared to be
anticipating that someone would pick her up—much the way
that you do when you want me to scoop you into my arms. The

statue was entitled "Come to Mom" and I knew I needed to have it in my collection. The pose is so you and the blue sweater symbolic of my little blue baby. The statue will always remind me of the devastating fear I felt today as I wandered alone in contemplation.

∽ MONDAY, MARCH 29, 1982

Darling Jill,

You came down with a viral flu today. I took you to Southdale Pediatrics. Your white blood count was 5000, which was indicative of a viral instead of a bacterial infection. Ali has had a temperature on and off for the last four days too. It appears to be the same infection with you. I gave you Baby Tylenol but your temp was still 101°, so I gave you a cool sponge bath, knowing that a heart baby can't tolerate as high a fever as a regular baby. Ali seems to be doing okay, but you have been fussy and need to be held. You are very blue today.

∽ TUESDAY, MARCH 30, 1982

Dearest Jill:

What a day it has been so far! Your temperature went up to 104° and has stayed there for three hours. You turned ashen gray and have been terribly lethargic, falling asleep even in the highchair. Even your facial expression shows signs of sickness with a glassy-eyed stare. You started getting worse midmorning and I called Dr. K, who told me to give you aspirin in addition to Tylenol and to sponge you off in a tepid tub.

After your tub bath, you got just a horrible color and started shivering, but your temp came down for a while. When we got to Southdale Pediatrics, your temp was back up to 104° even an hour after the aspirin. Your white blood count was only 7000, but they started you on an antibiotic because of a slightly red ear.

Two doctors looked at you, and then they called Dr. Katkov. He finally saw you this afternoon. Finally, your high fever broke and you appear to be through the worst.

I wrestled with my fear as I cared for you today. I knew I had to stay strong. Watching your body turn a deep, dark grayish color shivered my soul and the image will be embedded into my memory for a long time.

∽ WEDNESDAY, MARCH 31, 1982

Dear Jill,

You are much better. You are still cranky and need to be held, but you are holding your own. The fever continued through the night, wakening you three times. You are sweet and so sick.

∽ FRIDAY NIGHT, APRIL 2, 1982

My dearest little Jillsy:

I write to you now with tears in my eyes. It was just one year ago tonight that you were inside me for the last time. All day long I have had tears well up inside me. I have watched you and held you because I need to physically love you and protect you if that is at all possible. In some ways, I don't think you need my protection—I think you are one strong little girl. Thank God for that. You have to be a fighter to overcome all that you have since the day you were born.

Today while preparing for your first birthday celebration, I hated to see your first year come to an end. All of a sudden, you seem bigger and older than I want you to be. I am afraid of your heart surgery and fearful that this will be the only birthday we may share with you. I believe you are too strong to die, but I guess my optimism scares me too.

Everyday I look around my new house while Ali and Tony are in school and think how could I make it without you here with me? You are my little sunshine, my warmth, and my daily happiness. I love to look at you and hold you in my arms. You have such expressive eyes. My God, they seem so piercingly alive, as if they know what is really going to happen. I feel like I write the same words in this diary over and over. But each day that you do something—anything—I just have to capture it on paper and make it last forever.

Today for some reason you were exceptionally tired. You woke up crying and I needed to hold you until you fell asleep again. You slept on and off all day but I brought you downstairs this afternoon when both Ali and Tony arrived home from school. You got so excited to see them—and they you. They wrapped your birthday presents. Tony wrote his card: "Dear Jill, I love you and I hope your birthday is nice." Ali wrote an equally sentimental note. I know that they will suffer if anything happens to you.

It's Tony that I worry about the most. One day he gave you a potato chip and you threw up. Well, I screamed at him and scared him so much. He is so protective of you now. He will ask to be with you two or three or four times day. He gets your toys for you now, plays with you, and sings, "Pop goes the weasel" all the time. If you choke or spit up, he comes into me and says, "I didn't do it." God, I worry that if anything happens to you because it would hurt him so much. I do hope I would not be the cause of his blaming himself for anything.

Anyway, as I said earlier, you seemed so tired today. It upset me to see you play one minute and then put your head down on the floor to rest. You never cried at naptime or nighttime today. Each time you just looked at me with those wonderfully deep eyes. Then when I started to leave the room, you rolled over and picked up your little head to look at me. I would say, "Put your keppie down," and within minutes, you would be asleep.

You coughed a lot today, but I doubt you had a fever. You are taking antibiotics so the doctors told me you are covered against pneumonia and bronchitis. Rest well, little baby. Tomorrow is a big day for you—your first birthday. I hope it will be the first of many, many birthdays. You need your strength for tomorrow and every day until your surgery.

Tomorrow, on your first birthday, you will be "blessed" by Rabbi Shapiro. In a Jewish ceremony, he will bless you and give you your Hebrew name, Gila Aviva. Let's hope his blessing will work wonders along with modern medicine. More than that, I hope your inner strength will pull you through. Keep smiling your beautiful little smile, my love. You bring happiness to all of us. Bless you forever.

∽ APRIL 3, 1982

Jill Elizabeth Davis:

You are one year old today! Your weight is 18 pounds and your height is 30 inches. By everyone's standards your first birthday was a beautiful day. It was filled with love, happiness, laughter, smiles, friends, family, memories, expectations, hopes, dreams, silent fears, and real tears.

You slept through the night and woke up on your birthday with a bright disposition. You seemed sleepy during the day and took several naps, but by late afternoon when your dad came home early from the office, you were wide awake and ready to open birthday presents with Ali, Tony, your dad, and me. You got a *real* "Pop Goes the Weasel" Jack-in-the-box toy and you loved it! But I think your favorite present had to be the Mickey Mouse talking telephone that Tony picked out for you. You got so many cards and presents on your special day.

At 6:30 P.M. we had your evening birthday party and naming ceremony. The guests included the Rabbi and his wife, the two grandmas, your godparents, and the four of us. While we had cocktails, you played on the floor of the living room looking absolutely precious. You were so busy with your new toys, making faces, smiling, and watching the new "Pop Goes the Weasel" Jack-in-the-box pop out of his hiding place.

Once everyone was there, I held you and the rabbi stood between your dad and me to bless our daughter. He asked God for happiness, a good education, and a good marriage for you later in life. He had us all drink from a cup of wine, including you. Your dad and I each read part of a beautiful prayer that asked God to bless our daughter. Then Rabbi Shapiro gave you your Hebrew name as he explained that you were named for someone special (your paternal grandfather, Julius E. Davis), someone that we all cared about, and that through you, his memory would live on.

After his regular blessing, I asked the rabbi to give you an extra blessing for good health and he did. Each time he blessed you, he touched you lightly on your head, and you would shake your hand at him as if to say, "That's enough" or "bye-bye!" You were so funny and, of course, extremely cute. The blessing ceremony was very beautiful and meaningful.

While we all ate dinner, you went upstairs with Stephanie, a favorite babysitter. You were getting fussy and tired. But dinner was truly a special occasion. I had cooked all kinds of foods that my mother had taught me. Many were from the Jewish heritage cookbook and obviously planned for our guests, the rabbi and his wife. The table was set in pink and white—flowers and all. I had ordered them from a special florist that knew all about your heart condition. She went out of her way to design and deliver something pink, feminine and special.

After dinner, you sat on your dad's lap and smiled as we all sang "Happy Birthday." Your godmother blew out the candles and made a wish as we all secretly made our own wish that your heart surgery would be a success and that you would be with us on April 3, 1983, to celebrate another year of life.

All in all, it was a memorable day that I hated to see end. I wanted to keep you a baby forever, safely protected in my arms. But life goes on and we must face tomorrow. As the day draws to a close, your birthday is behind me and I now must get ready to face your surgery. I promise myself that I am going to do a lot of living and loving in these next six weeks.

☜ SUNDAY NIGHT, APRIL 18, 1982

My darling Jill:

As each day wears on, I want to record every last detail of your being—every smile, touch, sound, movement, even every breath of life. I feel like I am in a slow-motion depression. On one hand, I ache inside; the tears are so near the surface, ready to pop out any minute. I am selfishly impatient, terribly temperamental, easily distracted, and quite emotional. On the other hand, I must let you be loved by others too.

There are countless squeezes, games of "Pop Goes the Weasel" (We now just call it "Pop"), and lots of kisses scattered with "I Love You, Jill" hugs. Even as I write this diary, I am afraid that I will not remember everything that there is to remember about you.

Each morning you sit in your crib peering out between the rails to see who is coming to get you. Oftentimes, you will be sitting there talking, playing, or chewing on the little diaper cloths that we leave in your bed. When we come in, you get so excited and usually pop up to your knees in anticipation of being picked up.

During diaper changing time you will stretch your arms way up high over your head for our "Stretch" game. Lately you also take your feet in your hands and bang your toes together. Almost always you grab your rubber pants when I take them off, as if they, too, are something to play with.

Breakfast time has become more of a meal now that you love eating with a spoon. I can feed you fruit and cereal morning and night. We even add a vegetable course to the evening meal along with your fruit and bottle. Your eating began to improve at about eleven months old, but when you turned a year old, I saw a big improvement.

Jill, you love your Nilla Wafers! They are your most favorite treat. You nearly wiggle out of your seat to get one. I also started you on Cheerios this week, which turned out to be another successful finger food. You love eating with a spoon. Apricots and peaches are your favorite fruits! Our goal, of course, is to build up your calorie intake so you gain more weight before your surgery.

Since you turned a year old, you can mimic more sounds. But I haven't the faintest notion of the meaning of the majority of your words. You will say: "dada," "dahdee," "hi," "hiya," "data," "cake," "keys," "goooo," "ba," and "quack." But some of the sounds are meant for different words. You call Ali and Tony something consistently for their names, but I have not been able to produce the sound accurately myself. You can say "Jill" if you want to, but it sounds like "shjill." I have heard you say "hot" and "ma" although the latter is never uttered on command. You actually call your dad "dah-dee" when he comes home and he receives the clearest sounding "hi" as soon as you see his face. I also receive a "dada" when I come home.

Today you went for your first bike ride around the block in the child seat on the back of my bicycle. You loved it! The wind blew in your face and you kept looking around as if to never miss anything that passed us by. We stopped to see a dog, a new fascination for you (along with birds and squirrels). Earlier in the week when you went out on a stroller ride with Grandma Phyl, you also got incredibly excited by the sight of two dogs.

Mentally and physically you are still gaining in your development on a daily basis. You scoot around on the floor at high speeds, whip into a sitting position faster each day and even lift yourself up higher onto your knees, but that is more often in an effort to get picked up by me when the urge strikes you. You comprehend more games, commands, songs, and instructions and your memory seems to be lengthening. "Pop" is still your all-time favorite game, although "Ring around the Rosy" is growing in popularity. You stand and hold my hands for a moment until the songs says "And we all fall down" and then you do!

You manipulate toys better, and your fine-motor skills seem to be improving. You use your index finger to push buttons on the Mickey Mouse phone but you also use the whole receiver to bang on the buttons as well. Today you pushed shapes into their corresponding holes of the shape box for the first time.

One of your new favorite toys is the old Toddler Truck that Tony gave you. The seat of the truck lifts up (with other little objects inside), and you act so surprised as your inquisitive little fingers search inside for something new. Today you actually scooted halfway across the playroom to reach the Toddler Truck and it held your attention for a full half-hour. Ali and Tony also taught you a very funny game, "Beep-Beep our noses," which you adore! They give the command and you reach across to press the nose on each of your sibling's faces! All of your other games are old standards in the infant world (Peek-a-boo, Give me a kiss, waving bye-bye and How big is the baby?), but each one seems like a monumental triumph when you do it.

Earlier this week, your dad and I met with your doctor to discuss your open-heart surgery, which we decided to schedule here in Minneapolis at Children's Health Center, on May 19. Dr. Katkov, Dr. Blum, and even Dr. Helseth, the surgeon, were present. We met at the Life Support Unit (LSU) conference room at the hospital.

Dr. Helseth presented his point of view on how the correction should be done. He explained the difficulties of redirecting the blood flow, of changing the chambers of the heart from high pressure to low and vice versa. He talked about only doing a partial correction if you ran into trouble during the surgery, and he even talked about unforeseen problems that cause death in post-operative circumstances. It was terribly depressing to listen to him talk. It scared us terribly because he was speaking from experience and the reality of your surgery's complexity. At the same time, he gave you an excellent chance of surviving. This surgery is clearly much riskier than either of the other procedures you had when you were just a few days old. No child has ever survived your *exact* procedure but there is always hope that you will be the first.

Dr. Helseth and Dr. Katkov also talked about "profound hypothermia" a method by which the body is cooled to an incredibly low temperature to slow down or stop all bodily functions while the surgeon makes the actual repairs inside the heart. Even though they will be using the heart-lung machine, there can be a period of anywhere from ten minutes to one hour when the body is so cold that, the heart-lung machine is on hold and the entire body (lungs, brain, everything) lies in a state of limbo—almost as if it were dead. There are supposed to be no adverse effects from this, but we were emotionally overwhelmed by the description of how the whole surgical procedure is going to be conducted.

The intensive, critical forty-eight hours following the surgery are almost as important as the surgery itself. The lungs, kidneys, and other bodily functions are directly related to the heart, and therefore, they represent potential trouble spots during the post-op period.

The surgery itself, including the prep time, will take about six to seven hours beginning around eight o'clock in the morning on May 19. The first two days after will be crucial, but then the rest of the healing time and convalescent period will depend on you. Factors that will affect a successful outcome include how long you are on the respirator and your ability to take food. This will determine how long you remain in LSU; it could be anywhere from ten days to two weeks or perhaps longer if you struggle with your recovery. Overall, the doctors predicted that if the surgery goes well, we will see a pink baby right away, and our familiar, smiling, pretty Jill will be back at home in about a month's time.

⌘ SUNDAY, APRIL 25, 1982
DAYLIGHT SAVINGS TIME

Dear Jill:

We have literally worn you out in the last two days! Spring has sprung! It was 70° on Friday, 80° on Saturday and it was also beautiful today. We have been addicted to the lake—walking and biking around it daily, at least once. Yesterday I took you around on my bike and then your dad went around too. During our ride, you talked and looked at everything along the way. Halfway through my ride, you turned around to see two dogs that were passing and you even tickled the back of my pants with your little fingers to get my attention. But on your dad's ride, you just pooped out and fell asleep in the bike carrier with your head bobbing to the side like a little drunk! He had to reach behind and hold you up with one hand and hold the handlebars with the other!

Today, all five of us walked around the lake with you, the Madame, in your stroller. You were so busy looking all around and talking away. But halfway around we noticed you were bobbing your head again—sound asleep with your nose smashing against the front of the stroller. Finally we lay you down in the stroller and you slept all the way home.

My darling Jill, you love dogs! You call them "puppies" and say "bow-wow" for them and "quack-quack" for the ducks in the lake. Your newest phrase is "Da-ta" meaning "Don't touch" and you say this as you try to remove the bandage on your burned hand or when you are reaching up to take the barrette out of your hair! Today you managed to get it out but you watched for my reaction the whole time!

Two days ago, you pulled yourself up to a stand in the port-o-crib in the basement while I was doing the laundry. I turned around and there you were! You did it again today. Unfortunately, you appeared to be bluer after the struggle of pulling yourself up. My little sweetheart, there is a bittersweet reward to each little step you take.

∽ MONDAY, MAY 3, 1982

Dearest Jill:

You are thirteen months old today. You weigh 18 pounds 10 ounces. You had your picture taken today at home by our professional photographer who has been capturing your progress on film during the past year. We had pictures taken with your favorite toy, the "Pop Goes the Weasel" Jack-in-the-box. Your favorite food has become Cheerios, which you call "Os" and we even got a picture of you mouthing the word "O" with your mouth all puckered up. And, of course, you had to be eating them during the photo session.

You were dressed in a pretty pink dress with socks and no shoes. I dress you in pink as often as I can because the pink seems to offset the bluish tone of your skin. Unfortunately, today your bluish color was still clearly evident. But I can't wait to see the pictures. The photographer said we should be getting the proofs back in about two weeks—right before you go in for your surgery.

∽ MOTHER'S DAY: SUNDAY, MAY 9, 1982

Dear Jill:

How do I describe the feelings I had today? It was a day filled with a mumble-jumble of joy and tears, of happiness and depression and of contentment and fear. It was my first Mother's Day with all three of my children at home with me. Last year, Jill, you were still in the hospital. I have to believe that you, our precious little baby, will be with us next year. At times, I think you are stronger than all of us and more willing to fight to live.

✆ MONDAY NIGHT, MAY 10, 1982

Darling Jill:

It is ten o'clock in the evening—a melancholy time of day. It is so hard to believe that in just one week you, our precious little Jillsy, will be in the hospital. You are so dear. Every moment that I look at you, I could devour you. What is so special, is that you seem to respond to my every look. For instance, we will be riding in the car, you will be in your little car seat in the front seat, and I will look over at you and smile. You give a loving look right back at me with your eyes sparkling. Sometimes when I am in the car I have this feeling that your eyes are talking to me, as if you know something I don't. You give off a sense of inner knowledge—almost like a mystical all-knowing insightfulness. I wish you would talk to me and tell me what you're thinking about—I want to see behind those intense little eyes.

Lately, I get mixed feelings watching Ali and Tony play with you. I am not sure that they comprehend the significance of the surgery that is just a week away. They love you so much. They hug you, touch and kiss you and oftentimes, just talk to you. We never know what you are saying, but you talk back to them with such intensity. You even emphasize certain syllables like "da-TA" and then you crinkle up your nose. Jill, you are also beginning to use, what I affectionately call, your magic finger (the pointing index finger on your right hand). A few weeks ago, you pointed at your father and said "Da-dee." Then he taught you to point at yourself when he asks the question, "Where is Jill?" Now you will point to yourself when I ask the question, "Who does Mommy love?" And oh, yes—I do!

✆ TUESDAY, MAY 11, 1982

Dear Jill:

As I wrote last night, it seems that both your dad and I are trying to gather up each minute of time with you. Today he came
home early from the office to take you for a stroller walk around
the lake.

Earlier in the day I had finished up all my housework right
after lunch, so you, Tony, and I went back to the old house to
check on things there. (It still hasn't sold.) While we were there,
you crawled and scooted around, opened drawers and moved all
over. You really moved fast! We got home around two o'clock
and I put you in the stroller out in the front of our house so you
could watch all the activity at the lake. You sat there eating your
Os and drinking your bottle. You watched the people and dogs
go by. "Pup-py." It is so neat to watch you call things by name,
not just repeating the sounds and words we say.

Your favorite words seem to be "goo-KIE" for cookie and
"Da-Ta" for "Don't touch." You now say, "Hot" whenever I
take your bottle out of the microwave and "hi Da" or "Da-dee"
when your dad comes home. You will even point to him with
your magic finger. Of course, I still get the "Hi Da-dee" when I
come home too. I am determined to have you call me "Mama,"
but you seem to stubbornly refuse.

I am sitting outside now waiting for you and your dad to
return from your walk. It is gorgeous outside, about 70° and
sunny. You looked so cute today in a little pink dress with a pink
and white eyelet barrette with little ribbon streamers. You kept
putting your hand on the barrette all day, looking at me and saying "Da-ta" (mommy translation—Don't touch!) with a twinkle
in your eye. You are innocent and mischievous at the same time.

Ah, you finally arrived home. You are sound asleep in the
stroller and your dad admitted that while you slept, he sat down
on a park bench and just watched you sleep. Clearly he needed
his moments of solitude with you. You both are so cute together

and you play for the longest time with you sitting on your daddy's lap. Now when you play, you sing with him, or more correctly, you mimic his sounds and giggle at the same time.

Oh, God, how hard to believe that one week from tonight you will be in the hospital fighting for your life. What a life worth saving!

∽ WEDNESDAY, MAY 12, 1982

Darling Jill:

You are better today. You had a bit of a cold and a fever for the last few days. Your cold is almost gone now except for the stuffy nose. You have been sweating more than normal but are not crabby. If anything, you seem more cheerful and playful than you did earlier in the week. You took two naps today and seemed eager to play when your dad came home. You played in Ali's room tonight on the floor for about a half hour. You love to take stuff out of the drawers of a mini-chest that Ali has sitting on the floor. Inside are little hair barrettes and brushes. You are so cute, taking them out and attempting to put them in your hair.

Today you also took the placemats out of one of our kitchen drawers near where you were playing. You had the drawer open and the placemats on the floor in no time! Curious and playful would be an accurate way to describe you these days.

∽ FRIDAY, MAY 14, 1982

Jillsy:

It is getting harder and harder. I am constantly in a sad state of mind. I find myself crying all the time now, wanting to be with you, touching you and kissing you. Just loving you doesn't seem to be enough to wash away the fear. In fact, you woke up early this morning and just wanted to be held—it was almost as if you know what I am feeling.

Earlier today, you and I went to Grandma Babe's house where you played for about an hour. When you got tired, I brought you home, but you cried when I put you in your crib for a nap. So I held you in the rocking chair and you fell asleep in my arms. God, it felt good to hold you.

This afternoon I took you to the doctor for a checkup. Your weight is close to 19 pounds. This afternoon we took a walk with the other children. Tony pushed you in the stroller almost all the way around Lake of the Isles. You saw ducks and dogs and you ate two cookies before we got caught in the rain and had to run home at five o'clock. Daddy was home when we arrived. You played with him, played in your playpen, sat on my lap to drink your bottle, and then went to bed for the night.

⌗ SATURDAY, MAY 15, 1982

Dear Jill,

Your day started very early so you got in bed with mommy and daddy. You snuggled with both of us, talking a whole bunch—none of which we understood. You played in your playpen after breakfast and then I put you on the playroom floor where you discovered the toys in Tony's toy cupboard. Oh, what fun! When you got sleepy a little later, I put you back in bed for an early nap. You didn't cry, just talked yourself to sleep.

The mood around our house is incredibly dreary. I feel like we are running out of time. I ache and hurt and want to scream. In fact, I want to run away with you and hide from the reality of it all. I have never seen your dad so emotionally displaced before either. He is always so logical and prepared to deal with the facts at hand. With you, it is different.

⌒ SUNDAY, MAY 16, 1982

Dearest Jill,

It is early morning. It is all like a bad dream. It feels like both your dad and I are going through hell and we are carrying you with us. It's almost as though I have committed you to death because I am so scared that is what is going to happen. I go to sleep and wake up crying and thinking about you.

Yesterday, all day, while we loved you and enjoyed you, I just wanted to stretch out time and make it last forever. I wanted to record every movement, sound, and expression that you had. I want to memorize your face for posterity.

We sat outside on the front step in the sunshine all day. You had your "Os," a cookie, and a bottle. Mostly we just sat there looking at you. Because the time is drawing near and I am so frightened, I can't remember all the things you said or did. I just took lots of pictures of you in the sunshine.

You pointed to your dad whenever he rode up on his bicycle and you got so happy and excited to see him. You sat with him in a lounge chair and leaned back against his chest. Your straight, flyaway hair curled up for the first time today—two little curls that flipped up over each ear. You sat in your stroller and watched squirrels running up into the trees, looked at geese and called them "Gee," and glimpsed dogs running by the lake. Whenever you wanted to get out of your stroller, you made faces and stretched your arms up and out toward me. You brushed your own hair today (and ours!). Tony pushed you up and down the sidewalk in the stroller. You loved that.

The whole day you were alert, looking for things and moving at every sound. You watched all the people and the animals and you even remembered where we put things, like the bag of Cheerios that we had placed in the back of the stroller. You stood up in your playpen and stroller today. You love to stand and try to pull yourself up anywhere you can. You even "walked" half-way around the playpen holding onto the side rails, although you turned blue and were tired out from the major accomplishment.

You continue to talk with your eyes—eyes that are so bright and expressive. If anything should happen to you, I will always remember those glistening eyes and the pudgy little cheeks that glow right along with each expression. I am so glad that the photographer captured close up a picture of you looking at me with that mystical look in your eyes. No matter what, that picture will always be a favorite of mine.

Last night when I put you to bed, I couldn't help but cry. I held you so tight. I wanted you to be strong and to overcome your heart problems. I know it is up to you and you are the fighter and the strong one. I know that you have to fight for your survival. I tried to tell you that you can do it, but all I could do was cry.

Every moment right now is like a memorable gift. Out of the blue today, you looked up at me and said "Good girl." You puckered up your mouth to say it and all I could do was kiss it and say, "Yes, you are." Just now, when I said, "Who does Mommy love?" you answered, with a puckered smile: "Good girl." Yes, my love, you are.

⌒ MONDAY, MAY 17, 1982
CHILDREN'S HEALTH CENTER

Precious Jill:

It is 9:30 P.M. and we are in the hospital just a day away from your open-heart surgery. You woke up this morning about 7:30 A.M. and played with Ali for a little while. The whole family had breakfast together and then you played on your daddy's lap before he left to go to the office. You went with me to drive Ali and Tony to school and then we went to Dr. Blum's office for a pre-op physical exam. You weighed 19 pounds 4 ounces and were 30 ¾ inches long. When we got home, you took a nap, and then we left for Children's about noon.

Once at the hospital, we went through the admitting process and visited our nurse friends in LSU. You had a chest x-ray, and then we went up to the fourth floor to private room #4826. The nurses measured your height and weight again and discovered that you had a bit of a fever—100.2°. Early afternoon, Dr. Katkov arrived to draw blood. You cried extensively, so much so that the hair on your head was soaking wet from screaming. Because of your fever, they took a nose and throat culture to grow for the next twenty-four hours, but later your temp was down to just over 99°. Unfortunately, it was back up again this evening, so they started you on an antibiotic as a precaution. So far I miss the familiar faces from LSU, and you hate having your vital signs taken by the fourth floor nurses. But we were surprised by visits from Debby Cloud and Paula and Janet, your other favorite nurses and you did enjoy seeing them.

Tonight you played with me after your dinner and snuggled with me in my big oversized chair that will actually turn into a sleeper bed so that I can be with you every moment until your surgery on Wednesday morning. You cried when I put you in your hospital crib, and although you are slightly whimpering at this moment, I think you will be asleep soon. I didn't want to stop holding you, but I know you need your rest.

⌒ TUESDAY, MAY 18, 1982

Dear Jill:

You and I spent the whole day together here in the hospital. You hated having your vital signs taken, but you still played with me a lot today. The big news of the day: You took your first unassisted steps toward me in the hospital room! I was so proud of you. I clearly remember the day, many months ago, when the neurologist predicted that you would probably not walk normally because he felt you had cerebral palsy. I was so excited to see you walk that I almost cried with joy.

You sat on my lap in the big chair a lot today and we played all your favorite games, including "Twinkle Twinkle Little Star." While we sing the song, you do the motion of stars twinkling by wiggling your fingers back and forth. And then, of course, you put your hands way over your head when we sing the part "up above the world so high." You were using both of your hands equally well to do the motions!

Tonight, I had visits from both Dr. Waterbury, the anesthesiologist, and Dr. Helseth, the surgeon. Dr. Waterbury explained his role in the surgery—a very important role. I really like him and trust him and it was comforting to know he will be there. My visit from Dr. Helseth was a bit more emotional. He is a large man with a gentle spirit. I thanked him for helping to take care of you and asked him to go home and get a good night's sleep because the outcome of the surgery was in his hands.

As he held my hands and very humbly looked in my eyes, he said, "No, the outcome is not in my hands, it is in God's hands." We said good night and I came back into the hospital room where you are sleeping soundly.

I am finished writing in my journal and with the tears running down my face, and terrific fear in my heart, I know that I too, must go to sleep in preparation for the very important day tomorrow. I will face the day with fear in my heart but with the knowledge that your open-heart surgery is vital to your survival.

Sleep well, my precious baby. Bless you now and forever.

↝ MAY 21, 1982

My dearest Jill,

How do I begin to capture the emotions of the past two days? My heart is swollen with tears and an aching so severe that I am not sure the anguish will not torment me forever. This pain is like nothing I have ever felt before. And yet, there is a numbness and serenity seeping between the agony and the hurt.

The past forty-eight hours have been filled with elation and emotion. Moments of jubilant celebration were mixed with utter exhaustion and impatience. Your surgery lasted seven-and-a-half hours. The next two days lasted a lifetime.

It all began when I passed the warm, nestled child, who slept peacefully in my arms, to the surgical team, who silently waited near by. I released my protective hold on your life just moments before the operation was to begin. The gentle anesthesia had melted you into slumber and I kissed that beautiful sleeping face one last time. The warmth of your tender chubby cheeks will forever be on my lips as I remember that final kiss. Once you were carried out of sight, the desolation and emptiness pierced my heart. I bitterly fought against tears to maintain my composure. Your dad and I waited in tense silence for it all to be over.

I have no recollection of the seven hours of actual surgery, or of my thoughts and fears during that silent deadly time. I do, however, remember hearing you had made it through, determined and strong willed. Joyful glee filled the air as a sense of glory settled around us all. What sweet victory! We stood confident in the idea that you, always the fighter, had succeeded once more.

Later, when I saw you, I was shocked to see your frozen body and the mass of tubes and monitors. Your appearance was grotesquely bloated. The paralyzed, immobile state that was necessary for recovery eliminated all traces of the feminine, precious child I had hugged moments before the operation. The drug-induced paralysis was needed to help the heart heal after the trauma of surgical manipulation. Breathing tubes and monitoring devices were critical due to the fragility of your condition. Round-the-clock nurses stood by your bedside, touching and talking to you tenderly, encouraging me to do the same.

It took awhile, but eventually I was able to respond and talk to the inert form that lay beneath the tubes, wires, and beeping sounds. I whispered, "Hello, little Jillsy-bean. You are a good girl. You did a good job for Mommy. Come back to us, baby." I stood alone with my thoughts, for I knew enough to leave your father alone with his.

The day after surgery progressed quite well. Again the sense of triumph lingered around your bed inside the intensive care unit. Your surgeon seemed pleased but cautious, and your cardiologist, the more passionate of the two, seemed to float through the unit, elevated by his high hopes for your total recovery.

Remembering that no child had ever survived with your same heart defect, and that because of its complexity, the surgical procedure was highly experimental, we moved through each moment of recovery with an acute sense of anticipation.

I got pretty good at watching your monitors and learning the symbols of distress. Your nurses were once again like goddesses sent from above to protect you. They were attuned to your every need and cared for you with such compassion and finesse. Your father and I took turns "guarding" your bedside, just in case "something" would happen. Minutes dragged into hours, but the time never seemed monotonous or dull. There was so much activity focused on your well-being—intravenous tubes and catheters putting medicine in and pulling samples out. Heart rate and blood pressure readings were as ordinary and routine as the ticking of the clock.

Your nurses talked to you as if you were not only alive, but also alert. They gave you dignity as they changed your diaper, administered medicines, drew blood, or just stroked your sleeping head. Gentle conversations flowed from their lips in an effort to make you more comfortable and part of your own care. Their compassionate warmth reached out to you as if they were oblivious to your unconscious state. Their empathetic gestures seemed customary in a room full of inert patients.

I quickly learned that despite the coma-like state in which you were suspended, your mind could hear my voice and decipher the familiarity around you. I timidly began the familiar "Jillsy" dialogues at the encouragement of the intensive care nurses. I sang your favorite song, "Pop Goes the Weasel," and hoped, despite my shyness, that my tentative singing voice was really reaching you on a conscious level, giving you a familiar sense of home.

My one-sided conversations with you continued throughout the afternoon until it was time for me to go home to see your sister and brother, to cook dinner, and to shower before returning for what ultimately turned out to be a very long night. I remember cheerfully making a spaghetti dinner for Ali and Tony (funny how the spaghetti casserole looms so large in my memory on a day when other things were so desperately more important!). As I bustled around the kitchen cooking dinner, I recounted for Ali and Tony how well you were doing. They joyously listened to my proclamation: "Your sister is going to be fine." Those words still echo in my mind.

When I returned to the hospital, the nurses noticed that your blood pressure, which had been slipping on and off during the afternoon, was in fact again responding to the sound of my voice. They encouraged me to continue my playful chatter and to sing your favorite nursery rhymes to you some more. Assuming I would ultimately go home to sleep, they even suggested I make a tape of my songs and my voice talking to you so that when I left you would think I was still there by your side. The voice recognition seemed to keep your blood pressure up and stable, both of which were necessary for your post-op recovery.

It was later in the evening, about 10:30 P.M., after your dad had gone home for the night, that I remember your nurse staring at and questioning the accuracy of the heart monitor. I, too, had grown accustomed to watching the numbers and readings on the bedside equipment, and I was equally concerned by what I saw. Your blood pressure was dropping, more significantly than before. At first we thought there was something wrong with the monitor, but a second read proved that it was unfortunately accurate. Simultaneously checking your stats, the nurse asked if I was okay. They always seemed so proficient at the dual monitoring of mother and child. I assured your nurse that I was fine, despite the fact that I had begun an inner panic from my lack of understanding about what was wrong.

Your cardiologist was called and he raced back to the Life Support Unit; he ultimately stayed the remainder of the night. The hours passed slowly and yet quickly in commotion and although I don't remember much about that fuzzy time, I do vividly remember the first "Code Blue" that bellowed out of the PA system at about one o'clock in the morning. A Code Blue that announced your first heart arrest.

I am not sure I totally comprehended the severity of it all. I felt so alone watching your tiny body lay so still in the big white bed. There were many life-support mechanisms attached to you—beeping sounds and pulsating equipment meant to sustain your life while nurses and doctors fluttered around your bed.

About that same time, your nurses decided to call your dad and have him return to the hospital. They were, of course, calm and matter of fact as they suggested he might want to drive back to Children's. A frantic, frightened part of me, grabbed the phone from the calling nurse's hand and cried to your dad: "Come back to the hospital now—she is dying." Shortly thereafter I was totally reduced to tears and quivers as I stood in the hospital's front entry waiting for his return.

While I waited trembling in the front hallway of the hospital, another Code Blue screamed at me over the loud speaker, and I knew it was also meant for you. A Code Blue generally draws all "free" doctors to the unit to assist with the problem, and sure enough, an oncology specialist who had seen me many times before walked past me in the hall on his way from the Emergency Room to the Life Support Unit in response to the call. He took one look at me and changed his course. Instead of caring for you, he decided to care for me. I will never forget his big burly arms and tall stature embracing me as I sobbed in fear and desperation.

Interestingly enough, my tears stopped at the sight of your dad. In retrospect, I am sure I was afraid to show my weakness in front of him and I immediately adopted the stalwart persona that I kept for the remainder of the night.

The hours in the middle of the night are somewhat of a blur. Mostly I just sat and watched a team of specialists arrive at the bedside, talk about options, attempt different lifesaving procedures, and continue their constant attentive care. I wandered through the unit looking at other nurses who made this ominous care unit their daily choice of work. "How do you do this all the time?" My inquiry emanated from a place of sadness and disbelief that one could relive a dying scene over and over again.

The early morning hours brought with them a diminished sense of hope. Doctors were thinking of doing a bedside dialysis as your kidneys had started to fail along with your heart. New surgeons operated right there in an intensive last-ditch effort to save the weakening infant.

About six o'clock in the morning, I took it upon myself to begin calling family members to deliver what appeared to be a foregone conclusion. You were not going to survive. Amidst my tears and devastation for you, my mind went rushing back to Ali and Tony when I realized that the last words they heard were "Jill is going to make it—she will be coming home soon." There was no way I could allow you to die without warning them beforehand.

I tearfully called Lisa, our baby-sitter, who was staying at our house. She adored you and the other kids, so the conversation was chokingly spit out between bursts of pain. While I drove the fifteen minutes from the hospital to the house, she awoke the children and had them sitting obediently in the playroom waiting for my arrival. I don't remember my exact words, but my pain will forever be seared into my memory and theirs. Two little children, ages eight and five, who fought desperately to understand my words: "Jill is going to die."

I suggested to them that all we could do was pray. My best explanation that I could offer was the only one that made any sense to me as well: "Her heart is just not strong enough to help her get better after the long and difficult operation." Later we would simplify the explanation even more: "Her heart just pooped out." I don't really know how long I was at home, but I was magnetically drawn back to the hospital to be by your side. When I returned, I quietly sat by your intensive care bed on a corner stool, in disbelief that you were dying despite the frantic efforts of the medical team crowded around your bed. I don't even remember seeing your dad or feeling his presence—my eyes stayed glued on you.

I was still sitting on that obscure corner stool when, at about nine o'clock, your heart stopped beating on its own for the final time. I will never forget the tender, mechanical hands of Dr. Katkov as he desperately tried to pump life back into your body with the rhythmic movement of resuscitation. There was a deep silence surrounding the bed as everyone concentrated on the intensity of your every breath.

Twenty minutes of constant CPR still did not revive the little heart to beat on its own. The nurses and doctors gravely looked at us, the parents, for an answer of what to do. Your dad and I stood side-by-side, waiting tragically for the last vestiges of hope. It turned out that it had to be our decision of when to stop the revival efforts, and for quite some time, we were tearfully unable to let you go.

About 9:30 A.M., something inside me snapped. I screamed or cried out loud, "Stop!" I knew my action would be a final pronouncement of death, but I just wanted them all to leave my precious baby alone. I wanted what looked like painful useless pounding to stop and I wanted you to be at peace. Even as I write these words, my eyes blur up at the remembrance of those final moments. As the breath of defeat seeped out of all who attended you, my precious little Jill was pronounced dead at 9:30 A.M., Friday, May 21, 1982.

The curtains were drawn around you as the nurses performed their final act of care. They dressed you in the perfectly clean new baby pink pajamas that I had brought from home. They disengaged the wires and tubes so that you were finally free from monitors and beeping machines. Their mission was to prepare you for one last moment of tenderness and mothering. It was to be my last goodbye.

They gently placed your rigid form in my lap. I was left alone while I held you in my arms to embrace the finality of life. Your infant body was reminiscent of an empty shell. Your spirit and the life were gone. The child of mine was no more. You were stiff and serene—a victim of surgery and failure. The baby I had given birth to, and the child I had loved and cherished for so many days and nights, had drifted away.

I knew I needed to hold you for that final moment to say good-bye. I needed to finalize the knowledge that you had lost your valiant fight and left our lives. But I was truly unprepared for the intrinsic obligation that commanded me to lift you into my arms and kiss my love tenderly good-bye. When I held you in my arms for those final moments, I finally accepted the dichotomy of body and soul. Your spirit would be ever-present in my heart even though your lifeless form lay rigid in my arms.

The world stopped for that moment that I held you one last time. It was an unbearable scene that I never could have pictured or prepared for in advance. I needed to touch you and feel the release of your spirit from the lifeless form. I needed to bond with your soul forever.

Streaming tears blinded me as I placed you in Deb Cloud's arms and I choked back wrenching sobs as I left the intensive care unit for the last time. I didn't look back as you rested against Deb's breast, silently rocking in the hospital chair beside your empty bed. I didn't need to see you, for I knew you were safe in death, as you were in life, in her loving arms.

Jill, you will forever be in my heart. I will never forget the moments when your eyes searched mine in silence. You never uttered the word "Mama" just for me, in all of your thirteen months, and yet, I know we were united in unconditional love.

Jillsy, it is a love I will never forget. Somehow, my sadness and grief are couched inside this exceptional gift of love. You were my gift. Your tender time on earth was an opportunity for me to love perfectly, without judgment or error. Despite my agony and wrenching loss, I will be grateful for having you and I know that I have learned from loving you.

My tears are just superficial symbols of the deepest sorrow I have ever felt. I hang on so desperately to the images of your face, your warmth, and your delicate chatter—all cherished memories of our time together. I cannot envision waking without believing you are waiting for me in your crib. Oh, Jill, I am so afraid of tomorrow.

I know I must go to sleep now. Night draws near and begs me to surrender myself to unconsciousness. Sleep well, my precious one. I pray that your memory will sustain me and that thirteen months of treasured moments will last a lifetime.

PART II

Gift of Time

✆ MAY 20, 1985

My dearest Jill:

It has been three years since you passed away. I just lit the Yahrzeit Candle commemorating the anniversary of your death. Each year at sundown on the eve of the day preceding your death, we light the Jewish candle that burns for twenty-four hours, setting it side-by-side with your precious picture and a single pink rose. It gives me a dedicated time to reflect and to mourn your loss. Tonight I find myself reflecting on how life has changed since your death.

I have discovered the gift of time. Interestingly, memories are sweet and they continue to overshadow the macabre moments of loss. It feels as though I crawled out of the darkness three years ago, step-by-step, to painfully recreate a life without you. But now, in reflection, it seems like it all happened without any purposeful effort to discover life after loss.

I don't really remember the details of the first days after your death. I know that I couldn't drive home alone from the hospital the morning you died. The painful walk into our house to face Alicia and Tony were deadly moments. The rest of the day is a complete blur. I don't know whom I called, what I ate, whom I saw, or when I cried. I do remember waking up the next morning thinking it was all a bad dream and that you would magically appear in your crib. At the moment of wakefulness when I realized my mistaken perception, I buried my head and my heart under the darkness of the bedding to ease the intolerable pain.

The house was filled with perfunctory visitors, but the visit with the rabbi was memorable. I sat in the library describing for him the joy I had with you. I detailed my time and my nurturing attempts at healing your heart. His eulogy was magnificent and yet he only met you once. He spoke of you as a beautiful diamond that had been flawed. He told an ancient story of a time when a famous king had a diamond with a flaw that appeared to be beyond repair. It was not until a master jeweler figured out that he could carve the damaged diamond into a rose that the kingdom appreciated its unique beauty. I remember thinking that his story was special for me. Your damaged heart and many scars could not deter my love for you.

I remember only a few moments of the day following your death. Your dad and I went to the funeral home with a picture of you taken only weeks before your death so that I could instruct the morticians on how to care for you. I wanted you to be warm, so I had you wrapped in a blanket that my grandmother, Ma, had made for you. Your dad and I each gave the mortuary special toys and mementos that we wanted buried with you. I didn't want you to be cold or alone. I was adamant about how they needed to comb your hair. But now I don't even remember if you had your little pink barrette clipped on one side.

I asked your nurses to be your pallbearers. I couldn't imagine big hunky men assigned to the task of carrying your tiny casket to your final resting place. Instead that honor seemed to belong to those who had cared for you in life. Once you were placed in your casket, I was afraid to see you in the final state of death. My final good-bye was at the hospital when I held you in my arms. However, when you were brought to the Synagogue for the funeral service, I silently entered the Temple Sanctuary and knelt down by your closed casket to bless you and kiss your tender soul goodbye. I needed to be alone and I selfishly did not permit others to destroy my private moment.

I wept at the gravesite, and I remember the awful feeling of seeing your casket tip to one side as it was lowered into the ground. I have always wondered if your little body was scrunched from the tipsy event. Unfortunately my heart and soul were so singularly focused on you that I can't remember anyone else's grief or discomfort. I held Ali and Tony's hands and comforted them with hugs, but their sorrow remained their own. Your dad spent each day in a world of his own, his grief locked inside his macho masculinity. To this day he prefers to grieve in silence; our disparate thoughts helped carve a permanent chasm between us.

Life changed the moment you died, but it all began to whoosh forward when your father and I were driving on the freeway toward the cemetery to pick out your gravesite on the day you died. I will never forget the moment he asked me to have another baby. He missed you so. You had been the survivor—beating all the odds up until the end and then you were lost. Your death was such a monumental crushing of his power and personal dominance of the world. It was the one thing in his life that he could not control.

But I, the eternal maternal woman, craved more motherhood even before the moment of your loss. He surprised me with his request to have another baby, but I agreed without hesitation. I was soon blessed—within a month—with the gift of another baby growing inside me. Only your dad knew, but I silently carried my secret for five months before I shared the news with other family members and friends.

I won't diminish the agonizing moments of struggle to get beyond the grief of your death—but I have learned to dwell only on the positive as a way to energize and live. My pregnancy was a blessing and a joyful anticipation. It was never meant to be a replacement for you. Having another baby was purposeful—not meant to cover up your absence, but to bring the joy of life back into our family. We wanted Ali and Tony to share life with a healthy sibling and not let your illness and death overshadow the joy of having a baby in the house.

After you died, it took me a very long time to change your room in any way. I didn't want to touch your toys or move anything from how it had been when you were there. It felt as if there would be finality to your life if I put away your clothes and toys. Sometimes I went into your room just to feel the closeness of you and smell the luscious baby smell associated with your personal belongings.

About six months later I knew that I had to let go of the possessive feeling about your room. A new baby would be sleeping in your crib before too long and in no way did I want to diminish that baby's arrival with an overshadowing memory of you. I decorated the room with a heavenly theme of blue and white clouds, kind of a dual purpose in preparation for the new arrival. When people asked if I was afraid my new baby would be sick or have the same heart defect as you, I assured them that I was not afraid and then I made a joke. I told them that because the room was "heavenly," I would deal with whatever.

I hoped for a girl. But the rational side of my mind knew that a healthy baby was all that I really wanted. To prepare for "whatever" I made a mental commitment to have another boy. Then if I were fortunate enough to have another girl, I would not only be blessed but also surprised. I so desperately wanted another little girl, but knew that a "replacement Jill" would never be an answer for anguish. To compensate for the feminine urges swelling in my belly, I packed away your beautiful baby pink closet and prepared for a world of blue. I picked out a blue-and-white baby layette and a boy's name. "James Michael" was planned for late March 1983.

Miss Elizabeth Anne Davis was born on March 26, 1983. She burst forth into this world with a determination and personality unequaled to any of her siblings. She was my physical clone but born with her father's personality. Independence, stubborn spirit, and a survivor's instinct. She was an individual, determined to be born and to exist. Even if you had lived, I have absolute confidence that this child would have wiggled her way into the world anyway with such determination and command.

Elizabeth Anne entered the world right at the stroke of midnight in a command dynamic performance. The umbilical cord was wrapped around her neck as she had lain in a breech womb position several weeks prior to her birth. My overly cautious doctor scheduled a cesarean delivery on March 21, given the baby's inverted position.

I did not want a surgical birth—heaven forbid I should have a scar from a natural process of birthing. But then again, I loved the idea that something contrived and rewarding would happen on the twenty-first of a month to wipe out the stigma of your death exactly ten months before. When she finally arrived, it was on her own terms—not at the scheduled C-section time as planned. No, Elizabeth Anne (Bess) had turned around inside me right before her scheduled surgical arrival. The doctors actually sent me home from the hospital the morning that the C-section was scheduled. They instructed me to wait for nature to take its course. She waited five days, and then began pounding on the exit door in the early moments of Friday evening—just in time to transition a movie-night-out to a hospital-night-in.

As she slithered out of me, then rested on my abdomen, her complexion seemed ashen gray. Her color silenced the room. Immediately I saw failure, deprivation, sickness, and lifelessness. Fear clutched my heart. She failed her APGAR scores—the test for normal body functions such as respiration and color. She wasn't breathing and there was no vibrant sign of life. Within minutes, however, she bounced into the normal range and her pink little body showed signs of life.

Without a doubt, the first few minutes of her life remained the only questionable or scary time in Bess' early development. She was vibrant, tenacious, independent, and loving right from the start. Her early childhood was unique, but not because of a medical abnormality. On the contrary, she was raised in an atmosphere of total love and appreciation—valued and cherished for her mere existence.

Jill, the name *Elizabeth* Anne clearly honored your presence in our family, but her nickname, Bess, also captured the memory of my cherished grandmother, Bessie, who died while I was pregnant. Bess brought health and normalcy back into our family. The first two years of Bess' life passed uneventfully. As her parents, we loved her and relished every minute of her "normal" existence. The time flew by, as I had forgotten how easy it was to care for a healthy child. She slept, ate, and played with ease. Everyone, from her parents and siblings to her extended family and friends, marveled at her. She grew up in a cocoon of love and an aura of magnificence.

The family felt whole again. Life appeared to roll along at a normal pace, disguising any irregularities. Your dad continued his law practice, but he broke free from the large-firm environment to exercise his autonomy in his own private one-man firm. I believe that control was at the core of that decision. I should have seen that change as an omen of what was to come, but I was too wrapped up in my new life, spawned by your medical experiences at Minneapolis Children's Hospital.

In July 1982, following your death, I was asked to become a member of the Board of Directors for the Children's Hospital where you had been treated. It was an honor to say the least, but more of a catalytic spark that ignited my ambition and personal drive. I loved participating in the business world, side-by-side with people who wore suits and used their minds to earn money. Baking chocolate chip cookies and changing diapers had always been a symbol of domesticity for me, but after your death I discovered I wanted more in the way of a professional career.

I first went on the Board as a quality assurance advocate and parental stakeholder. I quickly learned that I had a lot to learn and was a ripe candidate for education. I visited with or participated on every committee of the hospital and loved every minute of my learning as well as the rewards of my contribution.

Bess even went with me to board meetings! She sat on the laps of doctors and played with their stethoscopes during the long meetings. Everyone seemed to know about you and about the beauty of having a healthy baby born into my life following your death. The real magnificence, for me, was the fact that people remembered you. On one hand, I was Jill's mom, but I was also on the cusp of becoming my own person for the first time in my life. Suddenly, I was not someone's daughter, someone's wife, or someone's mom.

Being the youngest member of the Board of Directors was a voluntary entry into the world of business and finance. The people intrigued me and the concepts presented at meetings captivated my attention. I quickly discovered that I had an unquenchable thirst to learn more so that I would not appear stupid about concepts I did not understand.

What I discovered during the three years after your death was a gift of enlightenment and a newfound awareness of myself. What I learned, the hard way, and with much pain and loneliness, was that for the ten years of marriage prior to your birth, I had relied on a husband to be more than the breadwinner and dominant figure in the household. He was my "everything"—emotionally, financially and physically. I never understood the deprecation that came with that choice.

Having grown up in the 1950s and 1960s, I had willingly accepted a chauvinistic view of marriage and adult womanhood: I opted for marriage instead of a career. Raising babies, baking chocolate chip cookies, hosting dinner parties, and being a volunteer became my personal goals in life. Having a husband who was not only the breadwinner but was also the singular decision-maker for the family was what I thought I wanted when I married at age nineteen. What I discovered in the past three years is that my personal goals are changing.

Even before your birth, I became bored with that type of existence. But I never strayed far from the domestic nest. I had been a committed volunteer, a part-time calligrapher, and a teacher of adult night school—all of which took a back seat to my full-time job as mom. But none of this prepared me for what life would be like as an independent, self-supporting woman. Suddenly, after your death, I realized that my former lifestyle did not fully meet my needs.

Yet it never occurred to me that having a professional life of my own (separate from my husband) was ever anything I really wanted or needed. I never considered being an equal contributor to the household expenses an option. I never imagined that I was capable of financial independence, nor did I realize that I was building up anger for my dependency and lack of personal income.

After your death, I suddenly was re-awakened to thoughts that contradicted the belief that being a wife and mother was enough. When I came home from board meetings, I was so excited to share information that I had learned with my husband, who happened to be a "Chairman of a hospital board" himself. Surprisingly, he did not delight in my acquisition of knowledge nor in my excitement about the business world. Needless to say, dinner-table conversation was squelched or reduced to daily household items of little consequence. And I was left feeling frustrated and angry.

So where did I get my emotional gratification during the times of personal unrest? I reverted back to the relationships that I built with colleagues at the hospital. Once again, it was through you, Jill, that I began to evolve out of a dependency on my marriage to satisfy my every need. Slowly but surely I began to seek out other people for my emotional support and personal recognition.

Perhaps the greatest eye-opener of how I needed more emotional support in my life came on a day when Bess, at two years old, needed minor surgery to place tubes in her chronically infected ears. There I was, suddenly back at Children's in a parental role (not as a board member, but as a mother). My new little daughter was having surgery. It was an eerie feeling of déjà vu.

As with all day-surgeries, Children's allowed me to walk back to the presurgical suite holding my baby. While she lay snuggled against me, the doctors anesthetized Bess. Suddenly she was sound asleep and totally inert in my arms. The emotionally gripping memory that swept over me at that moment was the remembrance of how you, Jill, had been whole and vibrant in my arms, then sound asleep and carried off to surgery—never to return alive again.

When Bess was taken from my arms on that cold January day, I suddenly froze in a memory of days past. Your dad experienced his own version of déjà vu and opted to walk away in an angry cold sweep of solitude. I, being the good wife and perpetual pleaser, let him go in private to absorb the moment of discomfort. What I discovered, however, was that there was no one left to console me. The experience lasted only a moment, but it was monumental in significance. For the first time in my adult, married life, I fully understood the effects of feeling so alone and unloved.

Jill, I came home from that day feeling desolate and empty. As a woman and compassionate giver of love, I realized that I didn't have reciprocity in my relationship. I wasn't sure where to go with this realization. I think I just cried. And for a long time, I kept the secret to myself.

This past year has been one of discovery. I have branched out in ways that felt selfish but were designed for self-preservation. I took a vacation alone. Wow! A challenge I thought I was too inhibited to do. I went to a health spa in Wisconsin for four days and three nights. My goal was body restoration because I had had two babies in two years. I worked out, dieted, and rejuvenated my energy. What surprised me, though, is that I also had an awakening of my spirit.

I found out that I LOVED being alone. I had my own goals and workout schedule planned. I felt so selfish! Every day was spent in luxury and self-absorption. The experience was so different from motherhood. But the real eye-opener came when I was talking with other resort guests about marriage and experiencing the world as a quasi-single person.

I spent hours talking with a handsome man about my life and my husband. I learned that I was looking at my marriage from the outside in and was not actually living it. I found out that I was so focused on "how we looked" as a married couple that I forgot to evaluate how I felt as a woman. What was most amazing to me was that this man intently *listened* to me for hours. I had not had that kind of interchange in years. There was chemistry, but no sexual exchange—it was more of an emotional connection. But nonetheless, it opened my eyes to that which I was missing. We parted friends, and as much as I didn't want to admit he was right about my marriage, I vowed to go home and make it last.

I did not want to destroy my marriage (even though I felt desperately unhappy), nor did I want to be a single woman raising three children alone. I vowed to work on my relationship and hopefully make it survive the test of time. To be honest, though, I knew in my heart that the only reason my husband came home each night with a "glimmer of excitement" in his eye was to see his newest baby, Bess! But for the short-term, that was okay. It gave me time to explore options.

Stepping off the airplane with altruistic goals, I felt a cold wind brush between us. Within five minutes of my arrival, he admonished me for something and my hope of an immediate marriage renewal was crushed. I was home less than an hour before I knew my intentions were one-sided. Call it lack of chemistry or pure mismatch—we were no longer destined to be together and I was not prepared to face that fact. I was paddling upstream and as much as I wanted to have a romantic, loving, reciprocal relationship with my husband, I wasn't sure that it could happen.

I set out on a mission—to learn more about myself. Uppermost in my mind was the goal of making a "midlife" marriage exciting and fulfilling. Counseling and self-exploration were the avenues I pursued. My husband said he didn't need therapy, but if I wanted to go get "fixed" he would consider working on the marriage. In a sea of tears at my annual exam with my regular physician, I asked for the name of a good marriage counselor. I told him in all honesty that I was scared and afraid to be alone. I told him I felt unloved and was questioning the idea of having an affair, which would have been strictly against my values. I wanted help in exploring my own needs and insecurities. Mostly, I wanted to find a way to save my marriage.

The sad part was I realized how often I sat in my room, alone, watching romantic dramas on television and crying for the sheer fact that I didn't have that kind of love in my life. In fact, my husband was oftentimes downstairs watching a hockey game and being alone by choice while I dreamed romantically of creating the movie drama for myself. It was lucky we had a very big house because in the months that stretched ahead, we began to live very separate lives.

I cried, I sought counseling and I lost weight. Most people thought I looked anorexic. I thought I looked great. And one summer day, when the scale finally said one hundred pounds (for my 5'4" frame), I celebrated by buying a big slice of chocolate decadence at the neighborhood French bakery. I was oblivious to the distraught condition of my body. I was merely obsessed with being thin and disregarded my health. I ran on nervous energy and one meal a day. I began to develop my own friends and started going out in the evening with them. I would come back home and sleep on the couch or in the guest bedroom to avoid any negative interactions. My nightclothes were often left outside the master bedroom door, indicating I wasn't welcome. Separate lives kept the peace, but it certainly didn't allow us to really work on our relationship. I wasn't sure where we were going, but I kept trying to keep us from moving further apart.

When I look back on these past three years, though, I feel that life has had a progression. It feels a bit chaotic right now, but I somehow know that I am on the cusp of discovery. My hope is that I will discover the secret to a happy marriage or a happy life. Time will have to tell.

⌒ SEPTEMBER 19, 1988

My dear Jill:

Time has a way of slipping away from us. It has been more than three years since I have written in my journal to you. Life has changed and so have I, since I ventured on a path of discovery. When I last wrote in this journal, I had the hope of resurrecting my marriage and re-creating a wholesome family unit. But my timing was a bit off. My marriage, it seems, had disintegrated more than I knew. The staleness permeated the household in a stifling manner that inhibited any joy of living. As it turned out, 1986 was a painful year.

During the course of the year, I turned to career counseling to search for a better understanding of myself and to seek answers for improving my marital situation. The counseling led me to several important conclusions. First, I didn't see myself as a worthwhile contributor to the marriage because I didn't earn money or have a full-time job. My self-esteem suffered and I was bored without intellectual stimulation. I had an insatiable desire for learning and I knew ultimately that I wanted to market myself for a full time career.

However, I valued motherhood and believed in staying home with my small children. Therefore, I needed to plan a course of action that would allow me to be with Bess until she was in school—yet I knew I needed personal growth experiences that would allow me to learn new things. Graduate business school appeared to provide me the perfect opportunity to do both.

Unfortunately, while I applied to business school, my marriage collapsed. After futile counseling, we relinquished all hope of resurrecting a salvageable pleasure from our coupling and your father and I split up for what I presumed was to be a trial separation.

My whole world suddenly changed in every possible way. At thirty-four years old, I started graduate school on the very day your dad moved out. I walked into the classroom early that Saturday morning, not knowing an asset from a liability. Tears were close to the surface and although I sat in the front row to drink in as much learning as I could, I tried to hide my personal devastation from the other students.

The divorce dragged on for two-and-a-half years, which was actually fine with me, given my reticence to being single. I was unequipped for single parenting (three children under the age of twelve) and I still had great fear about being financially on my own. The first six months of 1986 were emotionally draining, mostly because I fought to save the marriage. I went to a marriage counselor by myself.

I learned the hard way that my husband had no intention of coming back home. He put our house on the market and fully expected me to be gracious to potential buyers as they traipsed through my personal life, bedrooms and all. For six months I tried desperately to say and do all the right things that would make him come home again. But to no avail.

I eventually took steps to move forward myself, and amidst studying for graduate school classes and raising the children, I hired an attorney and started looking for a house for the three kids and me. By this time I was exhausted and emotionally drained. I was unaware that I was also anemic.

When I look back on it now, it seems that the events of that horrible time were rather humorous. Thank goodness I still had a clever side that found the joke in it all. When I found an old mansion that was being converted to condos, I got excited to think that one half of it would be designed just for me. Even though your dad had rejected my lawyer's settlement proposal several times, he did offer to buy me this wonderful new house. Fortunately, fate stepped in to protect my financial innocence. The condo, it turned out, was well beyond the means I would be able to afford as a divorced woman. But the sale was thwarted anyway when I started to hemorrhage while showing it to your father for his approval.

Frantically, I cleaned up the bathroom floor, excused myself, and embarrassed, rushed home to call my doctor. Hours later I was in the emergency room with my mother. Under the circumstances, I had left the three kids alone at home and found myself calling to check on them while lying on the exam table with my feet in stirrups! A mandatory hysterectomy ensued and once again I found myself managing it all on my own, literally hiring baby-sitters I hardly knew to watch the kids while I was in the hospital and recovering from surgery.

The six weeks of bed rest and home care eventually passed. I was back on my feet and, in my mother's words, better off. In her opinion the doctor had taken out the baby carriage and left the playpen! My take on the event was somewhat more pointed. Marriage, and all its agony, had really taken its toll on my body. Amidst the trauma of hemorrhaging, being anemic, and having a hysterectomy, I comically summed up that life was so tough that not only did I reach rock bottom, but also, with the latest turn of events, "the bottom had fallen out."

On August 1, 1986, which was our fifteenth wedding anniversary, I created a card for my husband that simply read: "August 1st—it's confusing! Do we celebrate fifteen years ago today when I moved in or six months ago today when you moved out?" I received absolutely no reaction to the card, not to mention any anniversary gift of any kind. In lieu of affection or nostalgia, my estranged husband came to the house to get his roller skates and demonstrated his independence by skating around the lake alone, leaving me to wonder what at all was worth salvaging in this marriage.

Within a few days, I filed for divorce, recognizing for the first time ever that my needs were also not being met by this forced coupling. I never looked back. The tears had already been shed; the sadness had already taken its toll on my body and my heart. I lost twenty pounds and a lot of self-esteem. I cried for the lost dreams and for the fear of perennial loneliness. I re-entered counseling, but this time, not to save my marriage but to save myself.

In many ways, divorce was harder to accept than your death, Jill. Unfortunately, I had a greater sense of responsibility for saving the marriage and thus suffered for my lack of ability to do just that. For my failure, I suffered guilt amidst the anger and self-deprecation. At first I was unable to see the benefits of divorce or even to visualize how I might be better off alone.

The last few years of marriage, after your death and Bess' birth, were extraordinarily lonely times. Your dad only came home to cuddle his precious new baby, and he rarely spoke of you or the reminders of your existence. While I reveled in my new status on the board of directors and all the symbolism of participating as a member of the business world, he never acknowledged my growth, my excitement, nor my accomplishments. Sadly, he would not even share my memories of you, for he handled grief in an isolated manner that included dismissal of all reminders of the loss.

Last evening, on the eve of my court date to conclude the divorce proceedings, Ali gave me a gift that sparked my passion for writing once again. I had asked for a journal called *The Woman's Journal.* I saw the book as a symbol of my divorce and my re-entry into life as an independent woman. I had hoped to write entries filled with hopes, dreams, frustrations, emotions, encounters, and experiences. I anticipated looking back one day and marveling at the experiences I had endured and the accomplishments that allowed me to truly become a woman of independent means.

Today, my court appearance to end my marriage, was a day filled with incredible emotions and energy. I really saw it as the first day of the rest of my life. No one emotion dominated my thoughts. I felt confident in my own ability to understand the divorce settlement agreement and as before, I attacked details of the document with an intellectual vengeance.

The courtroom made the divorce more real and austere than it had been and it intensified the magnitude of the day. I was satisfied with the terms of the settlement agreement; some parts were in my favor and some parts were a compromise to end the lengthy battle. I don't feel that I gave anything away, per se, and I am comfortable with the financial settlement even though there is clearly a drop in my household income. The difference is substantial enough that I know I must learn to budget and plan for my future while immediately controlling my expenses on a daily basis.

The settlement agreement gives me the opportunity to work and to improve my income status at any time. Since my employment can only be a positive asset to my future, and can never be considered as a variable of change in my economic circumstances, I have accepted the settlement to mean "The sky is the limit!" I have the freedom to be as much of a success as I am willing to be.

Your dad called late in the day to see how I was doing. I had mixed emotions about his call. It was a gesture of kindness, concern, and thoughtfulness, but also condescending. I wished for a clean break so I could emotionally get on with my life.

The marriage died a long time ago, but in the two years and eight months that we have been apart, I have learned a lot about the dynamics of my relationship with your dad, and about myself. I was very young when we married and very much in search of a dominant male figure upon whom I could rely. I came into the marriage without any real experience in relationships. As many women have done, I used my own parents' marriage as my role model, and subsequently repeated many of the same mistakes.

Now I realize that my marriage was unhealthy. I lived a life of trying to please another person before myself and as a result, swallowed my anger and disappointment many times in the course of our years together. I did not accept myself as an independent woman. Instead, I allowed my husband to dictate many elements of our life. As a result, I never blossomed into a person with confidence in her own ideas. Your dad's personality, it turned out, was a poison to my system, blocking my own growth and development. Now that the divorce is final, I don't want to live with him again or mesh my life with his, nor do I want to be subservient to any man again.

The court appearance today marked the death of dreams, not the end of a marriage. I cried only once when I took the witness stand to "prove up the divorce." I found it very sad to testify in open court that yes, Shawn Davis was my husband, because eighteen years ago when I met I him, I had envisioned a lifetime commitment to this man. I also cried when the judge asked if we had three children of the marriage, because in my heart I knew there had been four children—and you, Jill, in your own way were more a part of this divorce than the other three.

When I was asked if there had been an irretrievable breakdown of the marriage, with irreconcilable differences, I actually sat up straighter, smiled, and said "Yes." For at that moment I knew that I was a person unto herself. I wanted more than this marriage would ever offer me and more than anything, I wanted a relationship of interdependence and mutual respect. I wanted to be with a man only if there was friendship, caring, and love—not control and domination.

Actually, when your dad called me later, I was able to say to him that the marriage gave me my four children and the divorce gave me something I never had before—a chance to be my own person. The future is really now totally up to me. It is an adventure that I am eager to begin. I am finally able to see that the divorce has been a gift.

ᐣ JUNE 12, 1990

Dear Jill:

Once again so much has happened since I have written in your journal. There have been changes in my personal life, parenthood, my career, and a move! After the divorce was final in October 1988, time swooshed forward in an exciting and rapid motion. Where should I start with my stories?

I bought a new house. I called it my "Goldilocks House." Not too small nor too big (like the Lake of the Isles mansion), but just right for three kids and me. I was walking down the street one day and realized that I had envisioned this house for years. My realtor showed me the house after many others (all of which were not right for one reason or another—too small, too big, too expensive). This house was vacant and the empty rooms allowed me to imagine myself living there with the three children. The price was right and the moving in conditions perfect for someone who had no idea how to budget for major expenditures!

Alicia, Tony, and Bess would each have their own spacious room on the second floor. My goal was to ensure that the children did not feel like victims of divorce. As the oldest, Ali got the room with the phone line; Tony got the one with the TV connection; and Bess got the largest room because she would be there the longest. I bought the house with the intention of raising three kids there for thirteen years, until Bess graduated from high school. There was a wonderful family room off the kitchen, a big center island with bar stools for family dinners in the kitchen, a fireplace in the spacious old living room, and a formal dining room with elegant wood cupboards and antique décor. The most fun was the third floor, which I affectionately called "The Mastress Suite" (I was not the master of the house nor someone's mistress). It was a huge master bedroom with a very large office and a fully updated master bathroom complete with a Jacuzzi whirlpool tub, stall shower and a bidet!

I planned the move to the new house carefully so that I could manage graduate school, parenting, and a move by myself without too much stress. I took six weeks of time to move from Lake of the Isles after taking possession of the new house. That way, I could move a little bit each day, setting up house methodically and effortlessly. It was fun to have everything neatly put away in brand new cupboards, new spaces, and in what began to feel like a creative new lifestyle. The kids even told me that my whole demeanor shifted when I entered the new house—as though I had left my sorrow behind me. Personally, I felt a whole new world opening up to me. The new house represented a fresh beginning, a pathway to the future.

My life was becoming more fulfilling as I developed my own interests and pursued my own lifestyle. My days were filled with graduate school studies, hospital board meetings, a part-time job, and my regular duties as a mom. I took only one or two classes per semester (although I went to summer school), so that I didn't fall too far behind my plan to graduate by the time Bess was in school full time. I studied extensively (the kids said obsessively) and I was tenacious in my quest for a straight-A grade point average.

I was intellectually stimulated and fascinated by all that I was learning. I used the Children's Hospital as my prototype for understanding business concepts. I served on three related hospital boards and participated on as many different committees as I could to get exposed to a cross section of organizational concepts. I loved meeting new people and I built a strong network of contacts as I expanded my horizons. I voraciously networked in the business community, building a platform from which I would find a job when I graduated from business school. I appeared to be as organized in my life plan as I was in my new house.

While I was extremely absorbed in my own development and survival, the trials and tribulations of my children did not go unnoticed. The separation and divorce affected each of them in different ways and there were moments of excruciating pain. Sometimes, the events were out of my control, but looking back, I saw moments that helped define my strength and independence.

The devastation from your loss left painful scars on your brother, Tony. The most vivid memories of his fourth year were of you—moving in and out of hospitals and then dying. He suffered tremendously and silently for years following your death. I was extremely close to Tony, his ally and his savior in many ways. But he kept his sadness for you deep inside. However, at times, I served as the target for his anger, frustration, and pain.

His father did not seem to cope with Tony's tender moments or tears. There was a constant reminder of the painful differences between our styles of parenting every time Tony returned from weekends at his dad's house. At your dad's he couldn't express anything; at mine, he let it all out. We went through a few years of defiance and rebellion.

With Tony's precarious sensitivity, I lived through many screaming nights of his tears outside my door and his relentless call for help. There were countless sleepless nights. His sister died, his father left home, and he, being exceptionally bright but very young, struggled to piece together the explanation for your death and the destruction of his home as he knew it. I learned that the cognitive and the emotional development of a child were not always on a parallel path. Innately he knew so much and yet his chronological age prevented him from knowing what he needed to understand.

Tony's struggle ultimately led him away from the place where so much pain and anger pierced his soul and diminished his spirit. In 1988 he went away to boarding school to learn the hard way that he must cope with his own success and failure. While I loved him desperately, his emotional adjustment was beyond my control. One of the saddest days of my life was leaving my young son at the Connecticut boarding school alone amidst strangers. He was just eleven years old. Logically, I knew it was the right thing to do. Emotionally, I felt guilty and that I had failed him as a mother. My personal pain came not only from my feelings of inadequacy, but also from witnessing fear and uncertainty in my child's eyes.

The doctors demonstrated for me that I was his lifeline in the apparent absence of a father who rejected this exceptionally sensitive young man. The macho man apparently couldn't accept a young boy's tenderness or tears. In my opinion, verbally abusive behavior by his dad alienated the eleven-year-old boy to the point of causing what may be irreparable damage to their relationship. Tony's spirit has been temporarily broken; I look forward to the day it will rekindle.

Boarding school was suggested as a place where he could control his own environment amidst a more formal consistent structure. He didn't have to deal with the shuffling between Mom and Dad's house and he would be rewarded with extra time on vacations when there would be no academic expectations or responsibilities. The hope was that our home life would drastically improve, and Tony would adjust to being his own person, metaphorically in charge of himself.

The first year of his education at the boarding school had its moments, but overall I saw a remarkable improvement. Success was not without its trials and tribulations. Perhaps the most memorable and traumatic time was when Tony came home for Christmas vacation that first year. His holiday coincided with my move to the new house. As focused and determined as I was to move forward in my life, I did not predict that the transition from the old to new house would cause Tony great unhappiness and pain.

One night, amid shuffling of boxes and great chaos, Tony was distressed and upset, but I failed to notice. In a desperate moment, unbeknownst to me, he swallowed an entire bottle of his asthma medicine. As the evening hours progressed, his inner turmoil became more than he, at age eleven, could handle alone. His stomach pain led to tears and the realization he had done something seriously wrong. When unbearable nausea ensued, he came crying to me and confessed. Disbelieving the severity of the incident, I tried to calm him down with rational thought. I was panicked and emotional, not prepared to believe that such a serious incident had occurred to one of my children. I even called the Children's Hospital emergency room to ask for advice—anonymously, of course.

We ultimately went to the emergency room at Children's Hospital in the middle of the night to see if he was in any real danger or if he was just emotionally traumatized by all the whirl-wind changes in his life. I knew our moving to a new house and the total separation from family while at boarding school were difficult, but I was afraid I had underestimated their true effect. Tony's confession that night, coupled with his desperate cry for help, heightened my awareness that he needed more than I could provide. The course of events that evening enhanced my compassion and maternal protectiveness.

Unfortunately, while my heart ached for this little boy, I also had to battle the paternal side of the equation by dealing with an impassioned father (he met us at the emergency room) who did not appear to believe in the child's pain or that his depressive state could lead to the medication overdose. The combination of emotions accentuated the differences between us and increased the tension and drama of the night.

The next day the doctors advised that Tony spend a week in an inpatient adolescent care center for assessment and treatment of his emotional pain. Separation from his family at such a tender age, coupled with the unrelenting sadness of your death and the move to an unfamiliar house depleted his strength. I knew I was not emotionally equipped or competent to support my son at this moment. But in my heart I believed that although his dad didn't have great affection for Tony, he would be the stronger of the two parents and would know how to handle this crisis situation. The events that transpired in the next twenty-four hours proved me wrong on both counts.

When we took Tony to the inpatient hospital, he formally needed to be registered and signed in. He was not a willing participant in the events. I can't imagine any little boy at age eleven who wants to be told they *must* stay away from home in a hospital that looked austere, unfriendly, and totally foreign. But there was not an option. One of his parents had to sign the admission documents and simultaneously turn a deaf ear as they pulled a sorrowful little boy away to his private quarters.

With all the drama and heartache, I was still utterly shocked by the turn of events. At the final moments of closure on this traumatic moment in my son's life, his father chose to abruptly leave the hospital, citing "an important meeting that needed his attendance." The significance of this pronunciation escaped me until hours later when I sat tomblike at home, sipping on an icy cold Scotch to anesthetize my pain. The fact was appalling. My "strong" husband, and my savior for so many years, had proven to be weak in the moments that mattered most. Rather than accept responsibility for a child's pain and heartache or for a course of action that would restore his soul, he opted to leave.

My former husband's exodus at that moment in the hospital was the crowning victory in the awakening of my own strength. When I needed him most, he disappeared. When I needed someone to lean on, I discovered that in the rawest, most excruciating context of life, it was I who would have to be there for me in the end.

As it turned out, the week proved to be valuable for Tony. Doctors conferred with both parents and with Tony to determine how best to support a child who really didn't want to be at boarding school but who needed to be separated from the family trauma. It was not an easy week by any stretch of the imagination. I moved into my new house the day after Tony returned home and we all just tumbled along until January 1 when he returned to school.

I waited anxiously each day to see how he readjusted to being away from home, but the rest of the year was uneventful and actually fruitful. Tony had a superb relationship with his resident advisor, a man who flourished in the role of teacher, confidant, and friend. His advisor and I kept in close contact, and whenever possible, I supported Tony via phone calls and care packages from home.

Later that spring during my visit to school, Tony and I had a wonderful time together. A weekend totally dedicated to just us! His grades improved, he was actively involved in sports, and he had role models and mentors with whom he felt secure. When he came home for spring break and summer vacation, he felt free to just "be" at our house and enjoy life without scholastic structure. He clearly had matured during his months away and I, more than anyone, felt that the nurturing role models at school greatly helped to replace the lack of a dominant male figure in his life at home. There was a newfound peacefulness and joy in Tony's demeanor for the rest of that year.

Tony's feelings about his father and your death remained hidden in his heart and he only chose to uncover that pain in his creative writing and poetry. By all accounts though, we had triumphantly passed a painful hurdle that affected us all. Despite the anguish, I found that there was great learning in this episode of life. Buried deep inside the agony of sending my only son off to boarding school, and then leaving a fragile, scared child in seclusion at an adolescent hospital, was a gift for me: the gift of inner strength, something I possessed all along.

∽ AUGUST 23, 1990

My darling Jill:

I am leaving tomorrow to go to Cleveland, Ohio, for my twentieth year high school reunion. It's hard to believe that twenty years have passed since I was an eighteen-year-old teenager with dreams of love, marriage, and children swirling around in my youthful head. But here I stand today, a thirty-eight-year-old woman, in the prime of her regrowth, nervously preparing for the reminiscent journey. In many ways, I am more cognizant of my development and dreams now than I was at eighteen. This time, I have already had an opportunity to "practice" being an adult.

As I put my best clothes in the suitcase, I find myself taking inventory of my thirty-eight-year-old looks. Thanks to my friend, "The Divorce Diet," I am still sporting the same figure of those high school years. Thanks to my friend the beautician, I am not sporting the gray hairs caused by an aggravated divorce. Thanks to my parents, and a long line of good genes, I am gracefully aging with what appears to be a youthful glow.

I find myself taking inventory of my psyche. There is also a healthy dose of skepticism hidden inside the suitcase. I'm contemplating the question, "What have I accomplished in the years since high school?" Surely, birthing babies is wonderfully magnificent, but how does it compare to the Nobel Prize or some other academic or professional success that one of my high school peers might bring to the reunion? Nonetheless, at least I am finding some confidence in the fact that I will have not only three (make that four) babies to brag about on my scorecard, but a Bachelor of Science degree in education and a brand new Master's Degree in Business. To add icing on the cake, I am extremely excited because I accepted my very first full-time job last night! Thank goodness, I am not going to this reunion single AND unemployed.

Graduate business school turned out to be one of the best ways to boost my self-confidence and discover my professional persona. I learned that I loved learning! I discovered my academic competitive nature, my achievement orientation, and my passion for perfection. I learned that I devoured business concepts and was a noted nerd when it came to accounting and precision statistics. I drove my professors crazy when I asked a million questions to ensure my understanding and I made everyone crazy as I meticulously overstudied for each and every test.

My children heard more than once, "Be quiet, Mommy is studying" or "Mommy has a test tomorrow," and truth be known I was extremely selfish more times than not when it came to my singular focus. I had one goal that surpassed all others during the years of graduate school: to graduate with a 4.0 grade point average. To me, a straight A average and graduating at the top of my class would demonstrate to my prospective job market that despite my lack of experience, I was a quick learner, an intellectual performer with an achievement mentality.

I had a wonderful mentor during my graduate-school years whom I respected and admired for her own personal accomplishments and her ability to be honest and tough with me. Kathy had been a corporate Vice President, despite the fact that she had Multiple Sclerosis. The years of corporate stress and diminished lifestyle led Kathy to choose an alternative career. Around the time that you were born, Jill, Kathy opened an exotic floral shop in downtown Minneapolis. It was the first of its kind and a wonderful addition to the aesthetics of the designer community.

I met Kathy when I would order flowers at the Lake of the Isles home. While you were alive, I didn't go out to many places for fear of exposing you to germs and unnecessary illnesses. Kathy designed the flowers for the assorted dinner parties that I hosted for your dad's business but she also did the centerpieces and arrangements for your first birthday party, a unique and special event.

In the Jewish religion, there is usually a formal "naming" ceremony that anoints a baby with the blessings from the rabbi and the Lord. We chose to use your first birthday as the formal occasion to "name" you and bless you in the eyes of the Lord. I am sure that I recorded this special occasion in your baby journal. At the time, I probably didn't mention Kathy, who helped make everything pink and picture-perfect for me and my little blue baby. She clearly knew the significance of the occasion and everything was pink and white—flowers and table décor! Kathy brought the extraordinary centerpieces to our home and shared my sentiments about the significance of this day.

One month later, when you died, Kathy also hand-delivered a remembrance bouquet and sympathy arrangements to our home with tears in her eyes. We became friends and confidants in the moments that she handed me the baby bouquets.

I ended up going to work for Kathy, two days a week. A flower shop and its exotic blooming flowers was the perfect antidote to depression. Plus I learned so much from Kathy. She taught me about all types of flowers, how to care for them, and how to uniquely arrange them. But more than that, she became a professional mentor to me as I left her employ as a floral assistant to start graduate school. Because of her personal history and physical handicaps, she never let me wallow in self-pity for the perceived hardships of graduate school and quest for a professional career.

In my last year of grad school, I talked with Kathy about my insecurity surrounding my resume. Even with a graduating grade point average of 4.0, the fact remained that I would have no real work experience on my resume. By this time, Kathy had sold her business and returned to the corporate sector as a senior executive with a major health care company. She introduced me to several colleagues and I was ultimately hired on as an intern in my last year of school.

When I graduated in December 1989, at the age of thirty-seven, I hoped that I would have a job offer in hand. Unfortunately, I was inaugurated into the real world. I had so many interviews and so many rejections. I was told that I was unemployable, that I couldn't do a job because I didn't have any experience. I was even told that I was too glamorous to be taken seriously. I cried, I coped, and I dusted myself off and tried again and again after each demoralizing session in an interviewer's office.

I managed to secure a few consulting assignments (again thanks to my connection with Kathy) and I finally resorted to the unthinkable strategy—reading the want ads in the employment section of the Sunday paper. Everyone told me that there was no way I would find a job in the newspaper. I proved them wrong when one summer morning I spotted an ad for an Executive Director of a nonprofit Children's health care agency.

The job description seemed perfect for my situation. The organization was a ten-year-old charity that had been founded by a mother whose own child had succumbed to childhood leukemia. Her determination and a generous circle of friends founded an organization that hosted benefit events to raise money for Children's Cancer Charity at the University. They were magnificently successful for an entrepreneurial group and yet they had reached a point where professional management was a natural next step. Hence the advertisement in the newspaper.

As with most of my job inquiries, I was turned down for the position from the moment my resumé landed on the administrator's desk. When I called a week later to inquire about whether my resumé had been received, he informed me that, yes, they had received it, along with dozens of others, but that they had decided to interview other candidates who had more work experience than I.

I had heard those words many times before in my six-month job search. For some reason, I got up enough nerve to respond emphatically and confidently. In my heart I knew I was perfect for the job. I had worked in the nonprofit sector as a fundraiser and board member for the Children's Hospital for the past eight years; I understood the emotional ramifications of losing a child to disease, and I had a management degree firmly in hand. Who would be better suited to the delicacy of a volunteer organization focused on children's healthcare research than a mother who had lived the experience firsthand?

With desperation and defeat hidden in my back pocket, I pulled out the bravado necessary to respond to the administrator's objection. I simply said, "Thank you for your consideration. I understand your position of selecting other candidates before me. However, in my opinion, they have only one thing that I don't have in their historical experience: They got *paid* for what they did while I did my work as a volunteer." A week later, I was called in for the final round of interviews, and last night, as I began packing for my high school reunion, I got the call that confirmed I got the job!

As excited as I am, I must finish my packing. I have decided to take Bess with me to Cleveland so that she can meet my relatives. I have no idea what to expect from the reunion; it has been so long since I have connected with any of my childhood friends. Perhaps this is just one more milestone in my discovery quest. In less than twenty-four hours, I will visit my past. In less than two weeks, I will begin my future.

Jill, you will secretly be a part of both occasions. I will carry your memory with me to Cleveland, knowing that more than motherhood, divorce, and business school, you have influenced my life the most. Your death has helped shape me into the woman I am. I will always believe that you were the real reason I got the job as the Director of a children's charity. I know that you were with me in spirit when I interviewed and your presence in my heart gave me the confidence to reach for my dreams. You are the star that helped me shine.

✆ MAY 13, 1992

Dear Jill:

Today is Alicia's eighteenth birthday. In the last few years, Ali has proven to be the "other adult" in our household, beginning at the tender age of twelve. She sacrificed a bit of her youth to help me parent her siblings. She gave up many nights with her friends to baby-sit for Bess and Tony. Much of her time at home was helping with domestic chores. She never complained, and still to this day remains an exceptionally giving person. She kept her emotions inside, though, and one has to wonder what the personal price really was for such unselfish generosity.

Ali totally supported me through graduate school and now with my first "real" job. She drives Bess to and from school, stays with her until I get home and responds to Bess' multiple non-stop questions on a daily basis. Sometimes, in fact, I think Ali should be dubbed "Mom-2" for her role in raising Bess.

At times I have taken out my own frustrations on Ali. She seemed to absorb things without malice. She is dependable and available. Great availability for me, but I am not sure how it will affect her overall growing up. What I loved most was that because I needed her at home, she and her friends would "hang out" at my house for their evening get-togethers. It seemed like everyone knew that Ali needed to baby-sit the little sister, but I loved having her girlfriends visit.

Ali did well in her school courses and she never needed prompting from me to study or prepare for tests. Drama and

183

theatrical productions were her after-school passion that she shared with several close friends. She even helped Bess secure a small role in a senior play that was directed by Ali's friends. Bess was a mini-drama queen from the get-go and she loved being part of Ali's theatre friends' gatherings.

Meanwhile, I worked long hours. I was completely caught up in my new job. Since 1990, I threw myself into intense action—learning, organizing, achieving, and trying to prove myself. I was determined to be a successful career woman. At the time, I had one very singular focus and vision.

Working as a Director of the children's charity provided me with certain perks and benefits. At the same time, the position was a mismatch for my personal style and that caused me moments of consternation. When I was married, I was one of the "social volunteers" accepted as a member of the group. As an employee, my status changed. In my role as director, I feel more alienated and not accepted socially. But my career and financial security are more important at this point in my life.

Working for this organization allowed me to be associated with the University, providing me excellent benefits that increased my sense of security. The corporate fund-raising aspect of the job introduced me to major companies and the executives who ran them. But it was the marketing and public relations component of my role that ignited my passion and planted the seed that I might be ultimately more fulfilled as a marketing director or sales executive within the private business sector. I have put those dreams on hold for now for several reasons. Insecurity and fear that I won't be able to find another suitable position weighs heavily on my mind. But quality of life remains a more important reason of why a change would not be appropriate now.

The past year has been emotionally difficult for my family. In some ways, I have failed miserably as a mother while trying to prove myself as a businesswoman. Juggling motherhood and a career requires more maturity and finesse than I ever imagined. Emotionally a parent needs to be there for her children even in the midst of her own life stress. I have learned that now, but I learned it the hard way—after one of my children was hurt.

As with many other young women, Ali's high school years were sprinkled with emotional insecurities about dating and friendship. Her school had an unusually high social competitiveness and as a result, she appeared noncommunicative and sad at times. Except for her best girl friends and two guy friends with whom she confided, Ali spent most of her time alone, at home. Some of her melancholy was disguised by her duty to baby-sit for Bess, and I went unaware of her sadness for a while.

Ali was always the kind of kid who listened to what I said, and we often talked openly about drugs, alcohol, and sex. I would let her try alcohol at home and we agreed that drinking and driving were absolutely unacceptable. She was conservative in her dating and she shared with me that to her, making love was something special and worth waiting for the right relationship. With drinking and sexual experimentation happening around her, Ali stayed true to her convictions and was rewarded for it until Homecoming night of her senior year.

Ali and I had discussed the "after-party" at the home of one of her friends after the school homecoming dance. I gave her permission to go, provided that she call me when she arrived (which had to be before midnight) and once there, she would not leave until the morning, even if she opted not to drink. When she called, I thanked her for checking in and was secretly pleased that she had arrived safely and was with her good friends.

The night was like any other high school party with drinking and fun among friends and dating couples. Though Ali was at the home of one of her best male friends, she was not dating him or anyone else. In fact, she had talked with him many times about her desire to wait for a romantic involvement. I knew he really liked Ali and was attracted to her, but I thought he would always honor her wishes. The evening turned out to be a life-changing experience for Ali. She drank but decided to go to sleep when she had had enough. Unfortunately, he also drank too much and he did not take "no" for an answer with Ali as he had done in the past. Your sister lost more than a friend that night.

Ali came home the next morning and made no mention of the disturbing events of the previous evening. She suffered silently for four months. When she finally disclosed the details of her violation to me, she cried, saying that she hadn't wanted to bother me since I was so busy and wrapped up in my job. Once again, Ali was taking care of me instead of herself.

I did what I could to support her in the aftermath of the most difficult time in her life. I was so sad for my daughter and equally disappointed in myself for not being available to support her when she needed me most. We have become closer in some ways as a result of the incident and she continues to confide in me about her healing process. She no longer considers the boy a friend, but worse than that, the broken bonds of trust and friendship may have scarred her for years to come.

Jill, we have all learned from Ali's adversity. If you were here, I would have shared with you, as I did with both Tony and Bess, the lesson learned from her unfortunate episode. In the aftermath of Homecoming night, I saw my children pull closer together in a protective bond. As a parent, I don't always know the best way to prepare my children for adversity, and that is why I am grateful for the gift of love that siblings share when they look after each other.

Today, at eighteen years old, your sister is beginning to glow again. She is looking forward to going to college next year. I will miss her when she leaves for school in the fall. Ali is still the most giving and unselfish family member. I wish her happiness as she moves forward in her life. She deserves to receive the goodness she bestows on others. I pray that the gift of a new love will heal her heart and allow her to trust again.

✆ MARCH 4, 1994

Dear Jill:

At forty-two years old, it is time for me to "March forth!" I resigned my position at the Children's Cancer Charity today. This morning when I was pouring my morning coffee, I glanced at my "Page-a-day" calendar and the message read: "There are no mistakes in life, only learnings." The message has special meaning for me. While I am sad that my first full-time job wasn't more fulfilling or didn't last longer, the opportunity to work there was a growth experience and a gift.

This position was a perfect transitional job—it better prepared me to work in the corporate world. My previous experience included eight years as a nonprofit fund-raiser and volunteer for Children's Hospital. So I was able to quickly grasp the concepts associated with running a nonprofit organization. I was also passionate about the charity and the need to save children.

What was difficult for me, however, was my inability to co-exist in two worlds at once. I had expected that I could serve as the organization's manager while still being accepted into the social circle of the community volunteers. It was from my own high expectations that I plunged into disappointment when I wasn't welcomed into friendships with the organization's nucleus of women. I was not really accepted as a paid employee either, for it was an organization that was founded and run primarily by volunteers who worked for free.

This was a tough lesson for me to learn and I suffered in the privacy of my home. I vacillated between feelings of failure and pointed anger at those who didn't accept me or appreciate my altruistic efforts. As with divorce, I am learning that when a job ends, it usually means there is no longer a match between the parties. No need to blame, just move on and appreciate the lessons learned from the experience.

I learned a great deal about the business community and my professional aspirations in the past four years. I have better insight for my strengths and weaknesses as well as a better definition of my interests. I will probably seek a marketing position and I know that I would love to work downtown.

In my spare time I am writing marketing proposals for prospective clients and networking with people I have met in the last few years. I want to find another position. The fact that I am not working full-time right now gives me more time to spend with Bess and Tony (who has since moved home to finish high school). Patience is a virtue and I must take my time to find the right new opportunity. But having the summer off might be a gift in itself!

⌒ AUGUST 1995

Dear Jill:

It is summer again and this time I am into a new creative and fun venture! I have developed a business reading Tarot cards! Yes, you read that correctly—an urban, fourty-three-year-old woman with three children and an MBA is currently marketing herself as a Tarot card reader and numerology expert. Not only is it fun, I am also pretty good at it!

There really was an organized strategy behind what seemed to be a flimsy career idea. I had always loved going to psychics and Tarot card readers. During a vacation to Sausalito, California, in my graduate school years, I visited a wonderful spiritual bookstore and came across a book on the historic elements of the Tarot and its significance with women's spirituality. As with all my passionate hobbies, I began to read and study the Tarot with energized curiosity. I used my intellect, intuition, and analytical personality to investigate and devour the concepts.

I apprenticed with other Tarot card readers to "find my niche." One psychic, in particular, who I had visited many times for insightful readings, was instrumental in my quest to learn more. She always commented that I had a powerful intuitive nature. One day she called to ask if I would be her apprentice and help her read Tarot cards at parties and large gatherings. She trained me on her deck of cards and counseled me on using my intuition to do the readings. We were the hot attraction at several parties and I reveled in the enjoyment of doing something that I loved.

Once exposed to the idea of card-reading as a profession, and to supplement what she taught me, I bought different books on the subject of the Ancient Tarot and voraciously attacked what I was learning, dedicated to the principle "If you do what you love, the rest will follow." I purchased multiple decks of cards and several workbooks for using the Tarot as a personality indicator. I researched the historical meaning of the Tarot as it related to numerology. My analytical side was as strong as my intuitive nature. I shied away from linking myself to a voodooist mentality and I never believed that I could predict the future.

Instead, I built a database of historical meanings for each card and cross-referenced them with years of birth, ages, and astrological signs. Using mathematical plans, I compiled a personality profile for each client that detailed what their birth date meant in terms of the Tarot. I printed out a report of each client's summary and then I spent an hour with them elaborating on the meaning of each card. Summaries included descriptions of inner strengths, life challenges, natural tendencies, and patterns of behavior most often associated with their combination of birth day, year of birth, and astrological sign. I created marketing plans, mailing lists, and strategic concepts around my research of the Tarot. I used more analysis than I did intuition.

To me, the Tarot represented a method of understanding our innate qualities; it could be used to offer insights relative to our strengths, weaknesses, gifts, and challenges. I would often use the cards to center myself in a meditative state; the process of looking deep inside to assess my natural abilities and propensities offered me a feeling of spiritual growth.

Since early 1994, I purposely sought opportunities for introspection and personal growth. The conscious decision to become a professional Tarot card reader was actually a part of a yearlong sequence of intertwining events that were all focused on expanding my career and my personal development.

In summer 1994, I accepted a job as a marketing director for a small woman-owned public affairs firm. My role was somewhat undefined, but it involved business development and strategic marketing for what appeared to be an already successful business. Within three months, I discovered that I was in a position and environment that did not match my personal style. I was essentially a glorified secretary getting tremendous feedback on what I was always doing wrong. Hence, I went home each night feeling stupid, underutilized, and extremely unfulfilled. I didn't quit my job, but I began searching for new ways to grow that might also lead to a new work opportunity.

I had heard about a communitywide mentoring program for corporate women. I loved the idea of meeting new people, having a mentor and positioning myself to network for a new job. I applied to the program with the hope that a mentor would expose me to new opportunities and I could gain new skills to help me succeed in the corporate marketplace. Through a twist of fate, I was accepted in the program as a mentor instead of a mentee. This turn of events changed my life dramatically and I hungrily fell into the world of mentoring!

Mentoring is a very old phenomenon. I was unaware, however, that it had recently enjoyed a resurgence of importance, particularly in the business sector. I quickly learned that mentoring has secured its place within corporate and social domains where individuals actively seek guidance and structure for self-development. Corporate America, thirsty for ways to develop new leaders, has devoured the mentoring concepts and methods that have been in vogue in recent years. Formal mentoring was a very new concept to me, but it fascinated me nonetheless.

I had always sought out mentors in the informal sense. I looked for people who could serve as sounding boards, opinion givers, guidance counselors, and the like—people who naturally had the experience or intellect to offer me counsel. My mentors were spontaneous but valuable. My mentors changed as my needs expanded or restructured themselves. Each had special qualities and served special purposes for which they were well suited.

My most valuable mentors encouraged me to grow. They all had different backgrounds, characteristics and styles. Some nudged me forward raising the bar bit by bit; others pushed me aggressively to new heights. My tolerance for this gentle aggression and personal stretching exercise depended on several factors including the strength of the rapport and respect I had with my mentor. Trust was always a huge factor in my willingness to accept firm guidance, honest feedback, and strong suggestions.

My first introduction to formal mentoring with this program where I served as the mentor was different. I entered the experience reticent and somewhat skeptical that I would be a good mentor or that I would contribute to the development of my mentee, an extremely bright and competent woman. I was totally unprepared for the outgrowth of my mentoring experience. In the months that ensued, I found that I gained confidence, strength in leadership, and a whole new vitality. What I discovered as a mentor was a new formula for maximizing the experience.

I remember sitting with my mentee, listening to her self-evaluation for her own performance review. I was awed by her accomplishments and encouraged her to be confident and self-accepting of her abilities. I was the mentor, the voice of experience and the voice of reason! What happened next surprised me. I left the session reflecting on my own strengths and abilities, my own successes and the important principles that had served me well in my life. I began to listen to my own mentoring advice and sensitive messages.

In both situations, whether I was a mentee or a mentor, I was energized by conversations that involved living in possibilities. I was ignited by the power of dreams and the potential to reach for the stars. Following my own advice to my mentee, I was determined to live within my values. I was not receiving any form of success or reward in the marketing job, and hence, I knew that I had to make a change, and perhaps quit my job, if I were going to respect my own sense of self worth. A wise mentor counseled me to leave the job gracefully. And so earlier this spring that turned out to be my goal.

To my family's amazement, I reverted to a health excuse for my resignation. I didn't want to burn any bridges and while the job was not a match for my interest or skills, it *was* affecting my health. It may sound humorous, but the health problem I revealed was none other than that my "chakras" were misaligned! This didn't come out of the blue. My boss, the owner of the firm, had given me a book on women's health that emphasized the correlation between the mind and the body. The metaphysical overtone explained that pain and illness are symptoms of malfunctioning emotional needs. I analyzed what I read and applied it to my own life. The book correlated sections of the body with elements of pain. Lower back pain, which I experienced throughout my employment in this job, was associated with loss of control over one's life. Interesting correlation. The role I was filling in my current position was one that did not strengthen my self-esteem nor create an opportunity to grab hold of my life and reclaim my own destiny.

I read the book *Feel the Fear and Do it Anyway* as a means of helping me quit my job. I also read a book entitled *Do What You Love and the Money Will Follow*, and that is when I quit my job to become a Tarot card reader. I quit the job so gracefully that the company gave me not one, but two going-away parties and my former boss and the other co-owner of the company became two of my first Tarot card clients!

I used my fascination with Tarot cards to attend another empowerment workshop that utilized metaphysics, meditation, and affirmations to create reality from our dreams. I built a marketing plan for my new business, created a database of prospective clients, and taught myself new computer programs to support running a business from home. I even took out an ad in the Minnesota business magazine, *Corporate Report*, describing myself as a personal and business consultant. My conservative older brother (with a law degree and an MBA) commented that he thought the ad was creative, but was pleased that there was no mention of Tarot card reading in my business description! "Let's keep that as our little secret," he said.

I have steadily increased my customer base and had lots of fun exceeding people's expectations on how well I could describe them. Friends have purchased the readings as gifts for others and I have met a number of new and interesting people in the process. I have enjoyed freedom and flexibility of running my own business, especially with the spring and summer seasons coinciding with working from home.

I supplemented my business activity with a great deal of net-working. I went to lunch with friends, acquaintances, and new contacts. One such luncheon companion was the director of the mentoring program for which I had volunteered. I delighted in her enthusiasm for her work and jealously asked if I could do anything for their company just so I could be around the conta-gious spirit.

As it turned out, I ended up as a panel member on one of their monthly corporate presentations. The panel discussion centered on "Work and Life Balance." I was one of a panel of four very dif-ferent women. We each brought a distinct perspective on work and life balance. There was a committed corporate entrepreneur, a woman who clearly fit the family profile of "double income with kids." There was a single, never-married woman executive from a large retail chain, and also a lesbian who headed up a major non-profit organization. My role on the panel was to represent the divorced woman raising children while managing a career.

I remember entering the room and looking at the hundred women from Corporate America to whom I would present my story. Remembering that these women represented the high achieving, well-respected cult of tomorrow's leadership, I was really nervous. Despite the fact that I had placed an ad in *Corporate Report* for my little Tarot card business (classified as "personal and business consulting"), I was not prepared for my sense of inadequacy as I faced my fellow panelists and the audience. Knowing that their career tracks were years longer than mine and that their incomes in most cases were four times my current salary, I melted at the thought of standing tall and proud in their midst.

A hidden sense of strength helped me through my panic. Ultimately, when it was my turn to speak, I resorted to personal stuff...the real basics of my personal life. I talked about my kids—including you. I talked about setting goals and respecting life balance. About not going for the biggest salary if it meant sacrifice and time away from the kids. I talked about the support of my kids and the whole idea that during my MBA and job search years, my kids and their handwritten cards with words of encouragement were with me on every interview. I couldn't even comprehend the high-powered corporate drama most of the women in the audience experienced each business day, but I knew to speak from my heart and tell the story of how you, Jill, had been my gift of entry into the business world.

Several days later, the CEO of the mentoring company called me. After admitting that she cried during my portion of the panel, she invited me to lunch. Perplexed but intrigued, I decided to go even though I was fearful that now that she had found out I was unemployed, I would lose my volunteer status as a corporate mentor. But instead, lunch was fabulous! I don't ever remember enjoying myself so much for what turned out to be a job interview.

The CEO of the mentoring company needed a business development director to take her company to the national level. After listening to me at the panel presentation, she believed that I might be just the right person for the job. Her lunch invitation was the beginning of the exploration to find out if her intuition was right. Our lunch meeting led to a more formal interview with her COO the next week. As I pulled out of the parking lot of her office building that afternoon, I knew, without a shadow of a doubt, that I had found my next career opportunity. Despite my enjoyment of working alone, I loved growing professionally and challenging myself with new opportunities. As much as I loved the freedom of having my own business and playing with Tarot cards professionally, I couldn't resist joining the mentoring company as the Director of Business Development.

As a clever perk after I received my job offer, I created a complete numerical Tarot profile for the woman CEO of the company at which I was hired. Her husband was more than skeptical when he asked, "Your new director of business development wrote you a Tarot card personality profile?" But when she shared with him the insightful assessment, I think he was impressed. He told her that I described her to a tee! She agreed, which was high praise from a woman I hardly knew!

I will start the new job later this month after I take Tony to college. I hope to continue using Tarot card reading as a technique for personal enlightenment and as a fun hobby to share with friends and family. According to my most recent Tarot card reading, the new business development job is likely to offer me many satisfying rewards. The spiritual feeling that comes from Tarot card reading is analogous to the doctrine of "Trusting the Universe." This phenomenon brings me closer to you, Jill. When I don't know what tomorrow may bring, I look to the heavens for guidance, for patience or both. So, moments like this, I look forward to watching the future unfold.

⌾ MAY 1998

Dear Jill:

In all the times I have written to you, I have not shared anything about my life as a woman, my dating experiences or any romances that I have experienced since your death. The past ten years have included many interesting experiences. In many ways I feel that I have grown from an adolescent to a woman in just the past ten years.

My early dating experiences can be characterized as humorous adventures. Having married my first real boyfriend and lover, becoming single again at thirty-five years old was an eye-opener and a cold shock to my femininity! By the time I entered the dating world, I was a student in graduate school, and I guess you could say I became a student, of sorts, of the single marketplace.

In early September 1986, my social life consisted of evening classes at school, but by November, I ventured onto the social scene. Somehow, between dating and studying for my economics exams, I learned the laws of supply and demand. During the semester I learned how to use the research materials in the business library for information on Corporate America. And this is when I met Charlie. One night after class, I met a girlfriend for a drink at the Lobby Bar of the Hyatt Hotel in downtown Minneapolis. I wasn't going out much at the time, so even a quiet, out-of-the-way bar was exciting for me. As my friend and I sipped our drinks, I scanned the relatively empty room. Two men sat near-by. The visual surveillance was mutual and soon one of the men was trying to engage us in conversation by just using his eyes.

Inexperienced, but not shy, I just started talking. Before long, all four of us were sitting together. Charlie was the better-looking of the two and the one I liked. He was tall, 6'1", with black hair and dark eyes. He was somewhere around forty and had a slender build with an angular chiseled face. Charlie wore a dark suit and a white shirt, my first indication that we were talking to "Mr. Professional." Eventually, Charlie offered me the rest of his story.

He was the president of a candy company out of St. Louis and also a lawyer. I was actually delighted at the lawyer part; it gave me a reasonable reference point, having been married to one for fifteen years. Charlie was in Minneapolis to buy back ownership of his firm from a major snack food company that had bought him out several years before. It sounded like he was doing business with some very prominent corporate Minnesotans, but I was skeptical and had to be totally sure. My friend, it turned out, knew of Charlie's family. She had a summer home up in Brainerd, Minnesota, as did Charlie's parents. Karen later assured me it was a *very* nice house insinuating that "how much money Charlie had" was the primary question on my mind.

Actually, I was engaged in the whole pick-up process as long as it remained somewhat anonymous. Anonymous on my part, that is. I was brought up NOT to meet men in bars, and there I was, fresh out of the "marriage pen" meeting a man in a bar. His saving virtue, of course, was that Karen knew his family and that he did have a professional history. But when he asked for my phone number, my childhood upbringing won out, and I suggested he give me his business card instead.

This is when it got interesting. Charlie did not have a business card! I asked myself, "How could a professional, lawyer-type businessman, out of town on a major business deal, not have a business card?" "Not to worry," he said as he wrote his phone numbers down on a cocktail napkin for me. So I gained his phone numbers, and he lost credibility. And forever more, he would be known as "Cocktail Napkin Charlie."

I did call him long distance the next night—collect. He accepted the call, which was a point in his favor. The conversation lasted an hour and the connection between us appeared to be quite good. Naiveté set in for a brief moment. I thought life was going to be so easy, for I had met a nice, attractive, professional man soon after filing for divorce. Maybe I should have studied more economics at this point! I might have learned right away that there are many factors that influence outcomes in the marketplace. A little more education on my part might have taught me that just when you think you've got the right product, at the right price, you might have the wrong customer.

He called me every week for months, with a promise to visit Minneapolis where he would wine and dine me. But every time we had plans to be together, Charlie broke the date. Every time. So actually, I never saw dear Charlie again. Once, however, when I was studying in the business school library, I ran across Charlie's name in *America's Who's Who*. He really was the president of a publicly held company and had impressive business credentials as well. Charlie ended up being my first real dating lesson during my graduate school years.

After Charlie, dating took a back seat to my studies, to raising the family, and moving to the new house. There was a smattering of new dates, blind dates, and dumb dates. My girlfriends and I had names for some of my more outrageous dates. There was "Mr. Breakfast and Lunch" because he was unemployed and never took me to dinner. There was "The Walrus," a big guy with a huge nose and unattractive mustache. And I can't forget "White Bread," a man who was very nice but so nondescript. For a while I thought the "MBA" of graduate school meant, "Men, Boys and Assholes" and I had the uncanny misfortune of attracting all the wrong men. My one-date wonders were an incredibly insulting reflection on my apparent intelligence. While I got "As" in my college classes, I was flunking my course in dating.

I did have one great relationship for about a year right after the divorce was final. Michael was a friend and the complete antithesis to my husband. 6'4", lanky, beautifully built, and a confirmed bachelor, Michael had tousled brown hair, beautiful hands, big brown eyes, and a gorgeous mouth that professed passion. Plus, he was very bright and highly educated. He had two postgraduate degrees, a Masters in Psychology and an MBA, but he was a man who was not impressed with wealth or social status. He rode a BMW motorcycle and lived in a tiny unassuming apartment right behind my house on the lake. I think he got a kick out of visiting my home and being welcomed intimately into the luxurious surroundings. In truth, however, we became great friends.

Michael helped me with my grad school homework during the year we were together, he played hockey in the yard with Tony, bantered with Bess, and taught Ali how to parallel park the family car. He changed light bulbs in the nine-foot-ceiling rooms of the house, created a fun diversion for me on the weekends when the kids were away, and he took me to places I had never been. I visited jazz and blues clubs, biker's bars, and little out-of-the-way places that were not at all in my marital repertoire.

We also did wild and crazy things that felt so much more grown up than my previous dating dalliances. Michael was also very patient with me, in as much as I had not been with anyone other than my husband. Despite the fact that Michael and I were exactly the same age, we had traveled very different roads. He was a thirty-six-year-old bachelor with many worldly experiences and I was a fifteen-year veteran of diapers, home-baked chocolate chip cookies, and elegant dinner parties. But Michael helped me through some lonely and hard times, and introduced me to some new and exciting times.

I actually met Michael when he went jogging in front of my house. Immediately attracted to him, I struck up a silly conversation. For our first date, he came over to have some wine, and I was so nervous, I didn't let him into the house. Instead we sat on the front steps viewing the lake and sipping our wine. Ultimately, I did invite him to dinner and we began an exploration of French wine during the fall of that year. Many bottles of wine, dinners, and fireplaces later, we were lovers. The magic is still memorable.

But in reality, our match was not one that was meant to last. Convenience and a prescription for "just what the doctor ordered" was probably the best way to describe our year together. Truthfully, I liked to cook and Michael liked to eat. Perhaps you could say I was lonely and Michael was hungry. I wanted a friend and lover and he wanted no commitment or social awareness of our relationship. Ultimately we split up when I felt our peculiar union had lost its respectfulness and mutual commonality.

After Michael, I floundered in my dating selections. I even went through my "Biblical" period during which every wrong man that I dated for many months seemed to have a Biblical name. At times, I thought I was dating the twelve disciples: John, Peter, Paul, and Matthew. No one melted my heart until the final semester of graduate school when I really fell in love. His name was Paul, but he was different.

It was a dreary fall day and I was going to a committee meeting at the Children's Hospital Foundation. From the moment I entered the room, the gray atmosphere outside seemed to disappear and a personal fog lifted for me as well. He was tall, handsome, blond, and professional. His big eyes surveyed my face surreptitiously, but I could feel the connection without even knowing his name. There was chemistry and mystery. He nodded with a familiar acknowledgment as he passed me his business card. The meeting dissipated into a faded memory except for the electricity of his look.

Days later, I ran into him at the grocery store. Ali and Tony made fun of my awkwardness as I said hello and acted like a gawking schoolgirl. But he called. We went out to lunch at a restaurant called "Chez Paul" and I smiled at the coincidence. Lunch lasted three hours. He was charming, highly educated and yet there was a sensitive, warm, introspective side to him. We had a great deal in common and it turned out that he lived less than two blocks away. Our new friendship turned romantic within weeks. I felt more passion for Paul than I had ever before experienced. However, the electricity and mutuality were to be short lived. Paul had someone else in his life—a long-term girlfriend who lived in Chicago.

Needless to say, I tried to break up with Paul when I learned of his other love. He professed that I was truly the one for him and he made plans to go to Chicago to break it off with her. Innocent and hopeful, I waited one Sunday night for his return and the announcement that they were no longer together. His phone call finally came late Monday afternoon, and with it, his admission that he couldn't break it off with her. We tried to say good-bye, right then on the phone, but the tears led us back together a few more times. By Christmas, I did manage to let go and I told Paul I couldn't see him anymore. He promised to call me when he was free. I think I cried on and off for a year following that intense period. But I didn't socially see him again nor did I run into him (or her after she moved in with him) for a very long time.

Four years later, one Sunday afternoon, there I was at the grocery store checkout line when I looked up and unmistakably saw his magnificent image two counters away. I was shaken but curious, and I waited outside my car for him to walk by. I offered a meek hello and much to my amazement, he smiled and offered a full explanation of his current status. Most important, he was totally single; he had broken up with his long-time girlfriend, and she was living in California.

We went out for dinner and a movie that night and for several nights thereafter. I learned a great deal more about his previous relationship and what he had personally gone through in the years that we had been apart. Despite the number of years that it took for me to heal from our first encounter, I fell in love all over again. This time, I was sure, we would be together for a long-lasting union. Well, it lasted—for only a few months. Then she called him one night and wanted him back. He didn't waiver. He was on the next plane to see her in California.

We talked and saw each other several more times that summer. Ali pleaded with me to let him go, because "he made me sad." She clearly saw what I didn't.

I had fallen head over heels with a man who was undeniably linked to someone else. My emotions overshadowed my logic and nothing made much sense to me. He had told me that I was everything he had ever wanted and he especially liked that I was bright, independent, and employed. His other love was an unemployed woman who had cheated on him and depended on him for financial support; but she was the one with whom he had a long-term relationship. At the time, I couldn't understand why he chose her over me. He ultimately moved to California to be with her, and his absence helped me heal once again.

In the final analysis, I learned another important lesson. Reason and passion can simultaneously exist in affairs of the heart—even if they are on conflicting paths. When I finally let go of any hope of resurrecting the affair, I realized that Paul needed to be needed by a woman. While I was madly in love with him, I prided myself on my independence and self-sufficiency. Those qualities did not help him feel strong and fulfilled. On our last meeting together, one beautiful sunny autumn afternoon by the lake, he acknowledged his feelings of inadequacy and his require-ment to be the stronger mate in a romantic pairing. His words to me were of some solace. He generously complimented me one last time, and despite the sadness of a final parting, his words became a tender gift.

Well, darling daughter, I continued my life as a single woman for a long time without a significant relationship. I kept busy in my free time by going out with the kids for dinner or a movie, shopping and working out. I even hired a trainer to be more effective in my physical endeavors. Every Sunday morning I went to the gym just as others would go to church. I was religious about my weekly workout; I enjoyed not only the physical results but also the time spent with my trainer.

I called Gary my "fat-free" trainer for he didn't have an ounce of fat on him and was in tremendously good health. He tried to encourage me to mirror his healthy lifestyle, pushing me each week to increase weights or repetitions in each exercise. He was patient and complimentary of my attempts at body-building (although I often felt like a real wimp!) and he even patiently listened to my weekly banter on my social life or lack thereof.

Each Sunday morning I went over to the health club for my session. Sometimes I bounced in there with enthusiasm and other times I crawled in with the hope that weight training and aerobics would lift the heavy mood of yet another weekend alone. Despite the many people at the club, I went there for solitude and inner refreshment for my soul. No matter how I went into the club, I always left upbeat and cheerful.

On the Sunday before my birthday this year, I brought Ali with me to my workout. It was a fun outing that the two of us enjoyed. That morning, Gary was in a particularly cheery mood and I secretly wondered what he was up to. Toward the end of my workout, I lay awkwardly prone on the workout bench for a final stretching session when I caught sight of a very handsome tall man with distinguished gray hair walking toward us. He said "hi" to Gary and was introduced to an upside down me. Within minutes I learned he was another Gary-client and within a half-hour of his departure, I learned that Gary had preplanned the accidental meeting.

Jack was a fifty-year-old man who had just moved to Minneapolis from New York to start a new business. He had confided that he would like to meet a "nice woman" and Gary decided to play matchmaker as well as personal trainer. I reluctantly told Gary that he could give Jack my phone number, but secretly I had doubts that there was any hope that we would get together. Ali kept asking me why I was so negative, and I just muttered that my experience told me that it probably wouldn't work out. I really didn't think he would even call. But I was wrong. He called two days later. Thereafter, we referred to him as Gary's birthday present to me! Jack entered my life at an extraordinary time.

For my birthday, I received a new journal that had a wonderful message inscribed on the front cover. It read: *Today I will translate the reality of my dreams into my ordinary day—for extraordinary results.* As I began the new journal I wrote some interesting entries that described my thoughts about personal growth and love relationships. I had come to a place in my life where I wanted to remain single unless a relationship truly was rewarding or "icing on an already delicious cake." I was no longer searching for a boyfriend...instead I was searching for peace. On the night of my forty-sixth birthday I wrote the following journal entry:

A year of growth—transformation and perhaps painful growth for what lies ahead. Letting go of the past. Acceptance of what is. Life in balance. Peace.

Shortly thereafter, I went to a private health resort in Arizona that emphasized "Life in Balance." The health spa provided an environment for bringing life more fully into balance through self-awareness. Each activity was structured around the underlying principle of "mindfulness" and, as such, the health spa staff helped guests see things in their lives more clearly and more openly. I learned that you couldn't make radical changes in the pattern of your life until you begin to see yourself exactly as you are now. Meditation was a vehicle through which an individual can bring the mind to a state of tranquility and awareness—one of concentration and insight.

I spent the weekend relaxing in a restful environment. There was peacefulness wherever I went and I felt as if I were truly soaking up every minute of each present moment. I devoured meditation exercises and tips on achieving balance and I drank profuse amounts of water to cleanse my body and my soul. I loved being at this healthful resort and wanted to bring home the gentleness, sense of calm and quality of life that I had discovered there.

On the airplane home, as I prepared for reentry into the real world, I wrote another journal entry in my special book. It highlighted what I wanted for myself in terms of a relationship:

I want a loving friendship, something romantic but comfortable. I want laughter, intellect, tenderness, warmth, exploration, and joy. I want an inner connection with a soulmate: sensual connection with depth. Someone to share time with and with whom I can share family and personal growth. I want a relationship that is healthy, active, and fun. There needs to be a real connection between the two of us, but there has to be independence for each as well. I want a relationship that complements each person. The questions I ask myself include: How does a relationship help me learn about myself? How does a relationship complement who I am as an individual? How do we bring our personal walls and historic baggage to each new relationship and yet allowing for the exploration of being together?

Clearly, these excerpts were written with the remnants of my relationship with Paul lingering in my heart. I feared that my desire for independence was still too strong. And I wondered if my autonomous spirit and my attitude of not needing anything would get in the way of yet another union. The only way I was going to free myself from this fear was by living in the present. I finally resolved, on my plane ride home, to stop chasing the concept of peace. It would only be there for me when I let go of the need to capture it. Living for today was the only way for me to learn to live.

The month following my forty-sixth birthday was an awesome month of discovery. It was the first time in a long time that I felt fulfilled with a peaceful sense of calm embracing my heart. I felt satiated and happy, and I didn't need to control outcomes for tomorrow. I began to experience more excitement from just living. There were fewer planned, calculated conversations, less regret, and more acceptance of what is. I found myself doing less analysis of what I didn't know or couldn't control. There was clearly less need for perfection. I began to enjoy what was present in my life.

A good friend offered me words of advice that still hold true today. She said, "To thy own self be true. Jodi, you are who you are. You were not created for someone else's critique. You are learning acceptance of consequences (or rewards) by just being you. Your own vibrancy, sensuality, and energy are the power of your survival. Letting go of the fear of being someone others reject may be the freeing agent you need to move forward in your life. Let the Universe take care of checks and balances. What will be will be. The Universe gives you what you need at each moment. There is a powerful attraction and radiance in the truthfulness of being you. Only with that truthfulness will you attract your equal."

I found myself at a different place than I had ever been before. I was complacent. There was a peaceful acceptance of what is and what may be. I began to let go of that which I could not control and accept that which is. It felt wonderful to just *live* my life!

My desire for a loving relationship was based on a desire for respect, admiration, tenderness and caring. I wanted inter-dependency. I wanted to love a strong person, but someone who would also let me be strong. I wanted to love someone who was self-assured but whose vulnerabilities were attractive to me. I wanted it to be in a partnership. Equal whenever possible. I wanted love to be natural—not forced nor obligatory. I wanted a commitment to be shared not feared.

When I returned from my Arizona retreat, Jack and I began seeing each other almost every day. It was a different kind of relationship than I had ever experienced. He was beautifully tender, strong, and perceptive. He was definitive, thoughtful and purposeful. And yet he was flexible, giving and warm. I even found him tentative and sometimes perplexing. He appeared to know his own desires and plans, but at times, he seemed hesitant.

However, he says he is afraid of himself with me. He believes that I would be a distraction for his new life here in Minneapolis.

I sense a real hesitancy to commit to feeling again. He is a dichotomy of emotion. He is sincere and deep but keeps professing that dating just one woman frightens him. And yet he does not appear to be a "player" of the field. Meanwhile, we enjoy wonderfully exciting and passionate times together.

What attracted me the most to Jack was how he treated and responded to me. During our first few months together, he got a crash course in watching me be a parent, sister, and daughter. I had Bess home almost full-time and Jack and I spent a great deal of time around her. My mother was in the hospital in the early spring, so my brother flew into town to help me with her. Jack watched me deal with her doctors and the unexpected hospitalization. Sometimes when we thought we would have a quiet Sunday morning to ourselves, the phone never quit ringing and there I was—mother, sister, and daughter all at the same time I was enjoying a new relationship. He was trying to start a business and I was juggling job, motherhood, and my other family obligations. Our time alone was special, but our relationship did not exist in a vacuum away from the other pressures of life.

Now, after three months with this man, I feel pure enjoyment with Jack. I really like him and I like talking with him. I revel in his tenderness and caring; he is a more giving partner than anyone with whom I have been involved. We dance around the word "love" on occasion. I am much more reticent to say how I feel. I want to be sure that I love someone for who they are rather than for the fact that it is nice to be in love.

Best of all, it appears to be a two-way reciprocal feeling. I know that I am living, not controlling, this relationship. I am letting it unfold and deepen as a natural consequence of our feelings.

Jill, I am still against the idea of remarriage. My fear comes from the painful memories of divorce from your dad. I am, however, reevaluating the possibility of a lifetime partnership. Right now I question my feelings about a life commitment with Jack for the relationship is still quite young. For now, I am enjoying this wonderful relationship for what it is today.

ᨒ JULY 12, 1998

Dear Jill:

It is Sunday evening. I am quietly soaking in all of the feelings of the past few days. Each breath I take helps deepen my understanding. The calming air lessens the tension and confusion of my emotions. The month of July, in fact, has been like a cold-water assault on my peaceful sea of existence. I began the month fighting with Jack, which was unusual for our good-natured relationship. We had been out to dinner with friends of his and, in my opinion, he crossed the boundaries of privacy by sharing too much of my life with them. My otherwise loving personality turned sharp as I chastised him for the breach of promise. It was the first time our warm relationship chilled.

Then, a few days ago, while we were celebrating the 4th of July holiday with some friends on their boat, I fell and fractured my tailbone. I didn't know it at the time. After I fell backwards I just laughed off my clumsiness with a drink and a girlish giggle. But the next morning when I stepped out of bed, there was a searing pain that rose from my toes to my head. Each step intensified the pressure. Something was very wrong. When the normal dose of aspirin didn't relieve the pain, I went to a doctor for an x-ray and learned that the tiniest bone at the tip of my spine had been broken. Tiny bone—big pain. Judging by my mood the week following the accident, not only did I have a pain in the ass, but I apparently was one as well.

This painful incident was accentuated by another unusual circumstance. Your father suddenly got married! Ali, Tony, and

Bess were involved in the celebration, so Jack and I went away for the weekend to a little bed-and-breakfast on the river. It was an emotionally unsettling time because my feelings were so mixed up.

Logic held no place. I was no longer in love with your dad and I didn't care that he got married. I even liked the woman he chose very much. Since I was in my own relationship, I thought I would have basked in my tender loving feelings for Jack. On the contrary, I began to doubt my feelings for Jack. I treated him poorly the entire weekend. I criticized him, finding fault with everything he did and said. I wasn't sure if I was sabotaging the relationship or if it was dying a natural death. I knew that a part of me was even more determined to prove that I didn't need any man in my life. In any case, last Monday morning we decided to take a break from one another to let the air settle.

Jill, it is a confusing time for me. I am not sure how long Jack and I will be apart, or if we will get back together. I just know that I need my space and time alone. I am in sort of a melancholy mood as I write in this journal, but I am grateful for the peaceful time to contemplate my feelings. Tonight I embrace solitude as my gift.

⌘ SEPTEMBER 16, 1998

Darling Jill:

I don't know where the time goes. The last few months have been filled with stress, sadness, frustration and fear. But, in the final analysis, there has been growth. I wish I had written more regularly to capture the situations, conversations and discoveries more accurately.

In recent months, I have felt increasing pressure bubbling within me as different parts of my life collide and vie for my attention. Changes at work and transitions at my job have suddenly caused feelings of failure. There has been a reorganization of the company and a change in my responsibilities. With my new status, I am in uncharted territory. It doesn't seem to matter that our entrepreneurial company is going through rocky times of readjustment and growth (as many companies do), because I tend to personally absorb the negative effects of the change. In addition to the developments at work, I am still struggling with my feelings for Jack. The past few months have not been easy for us.

Last month I went to my doctor for an annual physical. I described for him the turbulent events of my life, and how I felt like I was tumbling around, drifting aimlessly. Furthermore, I felt that I had lost the ability to progressively move forward toward a final destination. My doctor suggested that I try an anti-depressant to calm my emotions and support me temporarily.

Through counseling, I discovered that I had finessed the ability to self-deprecate during difficult times. I used the recent events at work to reevaluate my abilities and to question my intuitive sense of what is right. Change is inevitable, particularly in a corporate environment. But dealing or coping with change takes strategic artistic ability and inner strength. The key, I have learned, is to possess a strong self-image that is not dependent on external events. Self-love, once again, remains the single most important survival skill in both professional and social arenas. Staying true to one's values and appreciating one's own strengths, needs, and boundaries are critical to staying afloat as the life tumbles into tough times.

Jill, as I write in this journal today, I feel that I am slowly emerging from the recent darkness. I can feel the lightness in the air. My relationship with Jack is slowing deepening, but I am aware that time will tell how well connected we are and if we are meant to be together as life partners. At work, I have weathered most of the storm, but am cognizant of the fact that additional change is inevitable as the company grows into its next stage of development.

Patience and continual self-awareness will be necessary to ride out this phase of my life. While many old patterns have emerged in my battle to endure, I know that self-esteem and positive self-image are ultimate companions. While I have a propensity for wanting "happy endings," I am only the author of my journal, not the decisive author of my life.

Jill, these past few months have reminded me that we often need to learn the same lesson over again. Each new experience brings with it a gift. At times, it is difficult to see the gift, especially when it is embedded in adversity. For now, I know not what the future brings. I only have the sanctuary of today and I must embrace it as a gift.

∽ DECEMBER 28, 1999

Dear Jill:

Today marks the end of an important phase in my life. It is a period during which I have experienced tremendous personal growth, intellectual fulfillment, personal and financial rewards that stretched beyond any preestablished goals. It was a time in my life when I felt invigorated and stimulated and challenged all at the same time. What began as a quest for self-development, led me to a pinnacle of leadership and corporate success. This chapter of my life didn't end as I would have liked, but with its twisted finish line comes a new appreciation for gifts of the unknown.

Jill, you may remember that in August 1995, I started the job with the mentoring company right after I took Tony to college. I only had Bess at home, but Ali was living in the neighborhood and if needed, she would stay with Bess when I had to travel for business. She was a Godsend and lifesaver, for my job included a great deal of travel out of town.

I was hired to be the Director of Business Development and my job was to help expand the Minnesota-based company nationally. Within the first year, we opened offices in Chicago and Dallas. I then began traveling to San Francisco to prepare for another new location. I loved the travel! I also thrived on the entrepreneurial challenge of opening new sites and developing new clients. The whole experience was also a phenomenal education on Corporate America. Our prospects and ultimate clients included primarily Fortune 500 companies and I found myself presenting to senior executives of organizations such as Sara Lee, Charles Schwab, Ford Motor Company, Texas Instruments, Williams-Sonoma, Quaker Oats, J. C. Penney, Ernst and Young, Deloitte-Touche, IBM, and others.

Initially, I was presenting the concept of women's mentoring and my job was to seek corporate sponsorship for a high-potential women's mentoring program in each city. Ultimately, I was drawn to the sale of a universal corporate mentoring program that could be utilized at every level of an organization and for any and all groups within the culture. The corporate sale was more complex and "solution-driven," which resonated with my analytical personality.

During the first two-and-a-half years with the company, there was great growth and corresponding opportunity for me. We went from one office to five and from six employees to fifty. Personally, I went from Business Development Director to Vice President and then ultimately to Senior Vice President, heading up one of two divisions of the company. My compensation and my confidence grew at decidedly accelerated rates. My rewards were many, and far more than the monetary gain.

For the first time in my career, I felt fulfilled and utilized for my natural talents. I was able to use my marketing and management skills; I used my creative abilities and my communication talents. I was so intellectually energized! I was always challenged in a positive way, and loved the travel, adventure, and creativity of developing an entrepreneurial entity. From the day I joined the company, I reported to the CEO and we became friends as well as business associates. I never lost sight, however, that her company came first and friendships second. All decisions were made on the value they achieved for the longevity and survival of the company.

For the most part, that philosophy served me well. I was not only a SVP and senior decision maker in the company, but in her absence, I was the company spokesperson with the media and corporate interviewers. I loved being the keynote speaker at corporate gatherings and national conferences. I adored the travel aspect, welcoming the solitude and exploration of different cities in the United States and Canada. I met wonderful people along the way, not the least of whom were the people I managed when I became the national sales manager for one division of the company. I made new friends and acquaintances and learned so much about myself, sales and management techniques, and the structure of Corporate America. There was great reward, both personal and financial, in our experiences.

Jill, it is sort of funny, looking back now, that I used my SVP title as an identity. I had gone from being someone's wife, to someone's mother, to a *title*. I spent so much time enjoying my professional and personal role in the business context. Little did I know that the secret to happiness was finding who I am in the total scheme of relationships, both personal and professional. But it was a great training ground. I recognized that there were great personal rewards to my position, and the title did not define my value.

The company grew and grew, almost exponentially. With the growth came many changes and some rough periods of adjustment. The summer of 1998, when I went on an antidepressant, was the beginning of those difficult times. The company needed infrastructure. Those of us who had built the organization from the ground floor up were affected by the lack of infrastructure. Slowly but surely as the emphasis of the company changed, including the leadership hierarchy, the roles and responsibilities of senior management changed as well. Ultimately, when the CEO chose to hire an executive to manage her day-to-day operations, many of us questioned our ability to remain loyal. I personally struggled with the decision—first, because I don't normally like any kind of change and second, because I had committed myself (in my heart) to this company for the remainder of my career.

So here I am, at a crossroads in my life, wishing I had all the answers that will serve me well in the years to come. I, of course, look for the gift in this situation and know in my heart that I have achieved so much more than I ever could have anticipated from the experience of a job that lasted four-plus years. The experience brought many gifts into my life.

Just this week I made a final decision to leave the company. For many months I wrestled with the thought of leaving—the conclusion was not an easy one. I loved being a part of this company. My heart was there and while I was not the business owner, I felt ownership for the company's mission and its success. Now that I am leaving, I have searched for what I have learned with this experience and what has come shining through the sadness of leaving.

Not only did I experience personal, professional, and financial success during my tenure with the company, but I also learned a new model for mentoring and, hence, I offer it here as a lesson in self-discovery, achievement, and living.

Mentors are gifts. Mentoring is a gift of conversations—conversations that create vision and that allow individuals to experience dreams as reality. Mentoring is simply powerful conversations. Conversation, in its simplicity, is merely listening and learning from each other. Conversations that allow diversity of thought and style explore possibility.

Mentoring is most powerful when the conversations transition us away from our status quo. Conversations can energize the future. Jill, when we think about our normal day, normal means routine and restraint. We live with daily pressures. A day can present challenges, chaos, confusion, and sometimes, competition. When we live with this pressure, we lose possibility. When we live within the confines of normality, we become resigned and limited and we may lose our ability to dream.

Mentoring conversations can help us regain our foothold on possibility. Powerful conversations with people we admire and respect can create passion, energy and creativity. I think about brainstorming conversations with friends—casual discussions about a mutual thought, difficulty, or prospective resolution that requires new energy and/or creativity. Powerful possibility usually results from the free-flowing exchange of ideas. Oftentimes, there is a bubbling over of excitement as we burst forth with new ideas. When there is an exchange of creativity and ideas are nurtured or refined by others, the dream gets expanded and more profound. The dream advances toward reality.

Mentoring also equates with confidentiality. When it is safe to dream and discuss, the ideas become free flowing and abundant. Confidential conversations build a foundation for dreaming. The strength of a solid mentoring foundation is built on trust. When we feel secure we share. Dreams, however, are often created in thin air—and we must have the confidence to know that there is a safety zone beneath the dream. Mentoring conversations can infuse the dream with stability and strength. A valuable mentor can support the notion that "if you can dream it, you can achieve it!" From dreams, we can build possibility and opportunity.

I am left with the realization that mentoring is a personal gift—customized and personalized to individual needs. Personal achievement and success are never accomplished alone. We utilize our resources to grow and gain. Mentors can be the solidarity amidst the chaos of personal growth. Advancement is often preceded by turbulence and questioning activity. Inner turmoil creates instability during which our foundation becomes shaky as we expand and explore new patterns. We test new behaviors, we explore new opportunities, and we adapt new strategies to produce new and different results.

The mentor can be the mirror against which we reflect and reform our ways. Within the context of trust, confidentiality, and safety, we can "try on" new behaviors to see the "fit." We can practice new strokes, much like the amateur golfer or tennis player does as he revises his swing under the tutelage of a trusted pro. Perfection is not the expectation. Courage and tenacity are, however, requirements for progress. The mentor must be nonjudgmental. If there is safety in exploration, there will be confidence in the quality of guidance. Probing for answers and free investigation of different processes then will yield different results. These strategies for growth can take us off-balance, momentarily increase our insecurity, and dampen our enthusiasm for progress. That's where a mentor can be most influential.

Jill, I have learned that the mentor can be the "North Star" in our future sky. He or she can be the lighthouse in the turbulent waters and the temperance in the storm. The secret of mentoring, however, lies with the mentee's ability to accept responsibility for piloting the course. It is ultimately *our* journey, our achievement, and our personal goals toward which we must direct our mentors. Hence, it is mandatory that we accept responsibility for steering the course. With mentors in our lives, Jill, we are never alone.

I am now looking to the heavens to guide me to the next opportunity—for I know not where I will land or how the future will play out. I am so much stronger and more experienced than I was five years ago and for that I am grateful. If I look at the decision to leave my current position as a "gift" then I must assume that opportunity is the next reward.

ॐ DECEMBER 31, 2000

Dear Jill:

Here I am at another New Year's Eve nestled by the fireplace reflecting on the whirlwind year that has just flown by. At times it was an emotional roller coaster with ups and downs, but other times I felt as if I were coasting on a path toward serenity. The complexity of events involved not only my career and my love life but elements of tenuous despair that seeped into my family life as well. At those times I felt as if I were clinging to a fragile raft that was whirling around in turbulent waters.

The turn of the century (from 1999 to 2000) brought with it tremendous media hype. As we approached Y2K, as it was called, we all bought into the magnificence of change and advancement of life. I, however, had ended one year with several disappointments and began the next with hesitation and reservation. Not the most delightful of celebrations, as you might imagine.

Jill, remember when I left the mentoring company during the Christmas holiday in 1999? The sadness in my heart was complicated by a sense of loyalty and hope that I could make the good times last forever. In order to move forward, I packed my emotions in a box just the same as I did the contents of my office.

One hour after submitting my resignation, I raced across town to St. Paul to sign an offer letter with an up-and-coming new business enterprise. I was joining an e-commerce company to work in the highly technical world of B2B business. I was joining dozens of others caught up in the hype of modern technology and ambition. I was also joining a national sales team composed of people almost half my age!

The headhunter who placed me there promised great financial rewards, stock options, and growth potential. I was entering a new era of business and a new phase in my professional life. First of all, I had finally achieved a professional reputation worthy of attention from the executive recruiter community. Second, I was moving into a more lucrative compensation package that included a signing bonus, a base salary, commission, and stock options. I was seduced by the dollars and the world of innovation.

The learning curve was steep, the pace exhausting, the competition tough, and the lifestyle exhilarating. Despite the fact that I had traded in my fancy Senior Vice President title and a gorgeous office for no title and a cubicle in a raggedy old building, I was too busy learning new acronyms and technological terms to notice.

I was part of a sales team that quickly bonded in an attempt to establish our company's prominence in an evolving business climate. I was usually on an airplane traveling coast-to-coast in luxury and eating in phenomenal restaurants in New York, San Francisco, and Dallas. Texas was my primary territory and I enjoyed the variations in culture between the different cities. I had relatives in Dallas, hated the humidity in Houston, loved the culture and ambiance of San Antonio, and made my one sale to a company in Amarillo.

The sale of a Web-based supply chain management solution was increasingly difficult to explain and differentiate amidst emerging competition. Additionally, I didn't feel the passion for this service as I had for mentoring. Without a technical background, I never achieved the confidence needed to sell the product that had a difficult-to-prove Return on Investment. We were never competently trained in the technology, nor did we have the operations support to demonstrate our capabilities to prospects, so the winter dragged on with decreasing enthusiasm.

At the same time that I was learning a new technical job, I was also grappling with confusing circumstances in my personal life. For others, the turn of the Millennium brought fireworks in a celebratory way. For me, it brought fiery sparks in another way. The Millennium brought a sense of "new age" spirit, but for me, it brought the death of a traditionalist's dreams. January 1, 2000, brought with it not only the major change in my career but also an electrically charged end to my relationship with Jack.

For the two years prior, I had the most rewarding, loving, and mutual relationship of my life. Jack was a man with whom I could have easily spent my remaining days. I was intent upon loving and caring for him for years to come, when—all of a sudden—he needed his proverbial "space" and asked that we take a break from our partnership.

As we approached the turn of the Millennium, a variety of signs should have prepared me for the full force of his New Year's message. In September I received a card that said: "No matter how long or short we are together, I will always love you." I wondered about the mention of "short" in the message but chose to ignore the implications. In November, even though he was invited to my house and his mother's home in New York, he chose to have Thanksgiving in Florida at the home of a friend. Between Thanksgiving and Christmas, he gave me an oversized elaborate golden angel with a note stating that "she would watch over me when he was not there."

Amidst his declarations that "you are everything I have ever wanted…you are beautiful, loving, and the person with whom I want to spend the rest of my life" came the ironic words, "I need my space…I need to do things I have never done…I need to take a pause in our relationship." It took me months and many, many tears to fully understand what that meant.

We spent the entire New Year's weekend together, toasting our love and the future, crying and making love as if we were trying to desperately mold every kiss and caress permanently into the fiber of our being. With each tear, I professed undying love and understanding for his difficulties and innocently promised to wait until he found whatever he was looking for. I existed under the flimsy veil of "if you love someone, set them free and if they are truly yours, they will come back to you."

Interestingly enough, I thought the timing of the separation was perfect, given my new enterprise as a "wild Web woman" selling e-commerce solutions in the state of Texas. I was on an airplane, and he had his freedom to sort out his inner space. Logically it made all the sense in the world. Emotionally, it made no sense at all and I was at the mercy of so many friends who said I was being stupid to put up with the arrangement.

Even my kids tried to tell me that I was not living as I taught them to live. I just thought that they didn't understand the unusual bond that Jack and I apparently had. Even though we had broken up, we spent every possible weekend together or at least Saturday nights and Sundays when we were both in town. I interpreted his need for space as a prerequisite for success for anyone starting a new company. I understood the pressure of being in a committed relationship while dealing with daily business pressures. I was his greatest supporter, even during the "pause," helping out at his company, sending him notes, cards, emails and gifts, along with countless demonstrations of "I care." My time on the road, in my mind, matched his time at work. Our time together, I thought, accounted for his only time off. I was proven wrong by February when the lies began along with my first sense of humiliation.

It was my daughter, Ali, who informed me of the first lie one Sunday morning. Her friends had seen him on a date at a black-tie benefit dinner the night before. I had assumed he was working—for that was what he had told me when I invited him over to have dinner with me. I was snuggled on the family room sofa drinking my morning coffee when I learned of his deceitfulness. The moment I heard the news, the hot steaming coffee drizzled painfully over my heart. My racing pulse overshadowed the lump in my throat as I dialed his home number but got no response. I frantically pulled on jeans and a sweatshirt, grabbed my car keys, and with blind fury drove the few miles to his apartment.

Disheveled, angry, and shaking miserably, I looked like a scene out of a passionate murder mystery. As I knocked repeatedly on his door, I don't even remember what I hoped would happen. Did I want to find him there? Alone? Or would it have been better to find his bed empty of all traces of treachery? When my knocking produced no response, I nervously placed my key in the lock. My hand and my heart were quivering simultaneously. Within seconds I was standing at the foot of his bed, yelling like a shrew.

Once he emerged from his deep slumber, he recognized that I had learned the truth from the night before and he did what he did so well—romanced me out of my fury. My tears were matched by his profuse apology for the betrayal and he successfully convinced me of his innocence, despite the illusion of duplicity. She meant nothing to him, it was not a date, he just accompanied her to the benefit event as a favor and he didn't tell me for fear it would hurt me. As I write this now, I can't imagine why I allowed his words to seep into my soul with any sort of conviction. I left his apartment emotionally drained, but not totally unscathed from the incident. I wanted to believe him and yet I wanted to uphold my own principles of honesty and trust.

Later that evening, I received the first of what would turn out to be many email letters from him. He carefully articulated his own pain for having hurt me despite his intentions to the contrary. His self-deprecation was intermixed with a fierce profession of his love for me. In time he hoped I would forgive him this one mistake. As I slipped into the cool comfort of my sheets, nestled alongside my faithful little dog, I let my emotions and the effects of his email fade into slumbering oblivion. But a tiny red flag stuck surreptitiously inside my heart.

The next few months went by without much change in any circumstance. I was still selling e-commerce solutions and sleeping with Jack on the weekends. Intuitively I knew both situations were wrong for me, but as the spring flowers popped up with their glorious cheerful energy, and the warm winds danced across the blue sky, I desperately wanted to take part in the romance of the season. As the beauty of the season swirled around me, I was unable to make definitive changes in my life. . By all outward appearances, I masterfully managed my circumstances, but in reality, I drifted through my days with silent burdens.

The drama of my relationship with Jack was quickly overshadowed by the death of a very close personal friend of mine. Dr. Harold Katkov, your cardiologist, succumbed to an unexpected deadly infection. His traumatic and untimely death gripped his immediate family. But his loss also sent tremors throughout the medical community and rippled into the hearts of so many families he had served.

Harold had become one of my best friends. During your long hospitalizations, he watched me and saw what I was unable to recognize: my inner strength. Ever since your death he was a staunch supporter of my independence and perseverance to be a woman unto myself. Not only was he my most trusted medical advisor but he also served as a surrogate spouse in moments of crisis many times through the years. He personally checked Bess when she was born to ensure that there was no heart problem, he advised me and supported me during Tony's emotional episodes, and he even helped with other family medical questions and referrals. Harold and his wife, Jean, were at my graduate school graduation and every major family celebration, including many Thanksgiving Dinners. I was truly thankful to have him in my life.

I was deeply touched when Jean asked me to speak at Harold's funeral. In theory, my role was that of a patient's mother, speaking on behalf of Harold's compassionate care of his patients. In reality, I was speaking as a woman and friend who had benefited from almost twenty years of this wonderful man in her family's life. As I said at the funeral, when his babies were doing well, Harold floated through the Intensive Care unit as if angels had lifted him up in glory. But when his little heart babies were failing, a bit of Harold failed with them.

For me, he helped keep your memory alive and he gave wisdom to your death. He always said that as a result of watching me with you, he saw my strength and my capabilities. His belief in me was a powerful motivator and his presence in my life was a genuine gift.

Harold's influence in my life was extended after his death by my continued friendship with Jean, his widow, and Hal, his son. Interestingly, it was Hal, who in the past several months has had the greatest impact on helping me see the deficiency in my relationship with Jack. It was Hal who pointed out the error of my ways when he kept asking me to look inside myself for the real reason why I stayed with a man who lied to me. The question simmered inside of me.

As spring turned into summer, I continued functioning in my job despite my lack of enthusiasm or confidence in the company. Tony graduated from college and came home to begin his career in the restaurant industry. He had received offers from three well-respected local companies and when he accepted his first choice, we had a congratulatory party to celebrate. Ali was doing well at her teaching job in a St. Paul elementary school and had begun to date a fellow teacher during the year. She seemed happy with her friends and her life and I was genuinely pleased for her. Bess spent the summer before her senior year of high school with a part-time job and a full-time social life. She had an adventurous, independent spirit. We lived in the same house but rarely spent time together and I missed her.

The summer also brought with it the full disclosure that Jack was seeing someone else. My trust in him was irrevocably broken when my self-worth took a final beating. I felt humiliated publicly. My friends tried to tell me (some even called to give me detailed descriptions of their sightings), but it wasn't until I personally witnessed their affectionate kissing and warm embrace that I believed it for myself.

Jack had broken the bond of trust. He had been a good man—tender, affectionate, generous and caring. But in the final days of our relationship, his lies and betrayal overshadowed his goodness.

The pain I experienced when I realized it was over was like an old familiar, heavy woolen blanket. The weight was oppressive and I gasped for air. I needed to breathe molecules of hope to survive. But in the darkness, I never blamed myself like I had with my divorce. Instead, a dispassionate emptiness displaced anger and depression. This time there was a biting raw pain that gnawed at my insides and eroded my altruistic sense of goodness. Unfortunately, I battled the urge to lose faith in all of mankind.

During the summer months, I spent hours alone in the darkness. Late at night or in the early dawn, I sat on my front porch, drinking wine, smoking a cigarette, or just questioning the stars in the sky. There was a dull ache that just didn't want to subside and tears rolled down my cheeks without reason.

In the midst of my mourning, I suddenly found myself at the doctor's office for a nonroutine exam. The week before I had visited my doctor for a regular checkup. I was just making sure that my body was in better shape than my broken heart. It was during that visit that my doctor found suspicious signs of a potential cancer. Within a week I was scheduled for an invasive exam to confirm or deny the diagnosis.

Suddenly my midnight moods drifted away from the loss of a lover and settled more emphatically on what it would be like to die before my time. The loss of opportunity to watch my children marry or to experience grandparenthood became the uppermost fears in my mind. The cancer turned out to be non-existent, but the wake-up call moved me off the raft that was drifting aimlessly in melancholy waters.

Soon after, I got the urge to be more purposeful in my quest for serenity. I resolved to stay focused on a solitary path toward my personal goals—even if that meant I would be alone without a relationship. In my heart I knew that life had intrinsic rewards for living in peace and I vowed to steady my course with the truly important things in life: family, friends, and peace of mind.

As I sit here by the fire on the eve of another year, I gaze at the reflections of time past. The fire before my eyes sparks a desire to survive and go forth. The smoldering embers of the burning log simply dissolve the recent pain into ash. Hidden between the flames are the gifts that emerged despite the storm. I am drifting now on a peaceful sea. I am watching my children claim their own lives by spreading their wings and soaring into separate worlds. With Bess graduating from high school next spring, it is time for me to command my own destiny. I must create my own realm for contentment. Jill, next spring it will be twenty years since you were born—it is time to find my peace alone.

∽ AUGUST 1, 2001

Dear Jill:

Today would have been my thirtieth wedding anniversary. Seems like a lifetime ago that I began this diary to you, my darling Jill. August 1, 1980. The years float by as if we are in passage together on a magnificent voyage...but the destination is still unknown. I find myself at an exciting time of my life. I call it my Sentient time. It is a time for awareness and growth. It is time for stretching my wings with a new sense of freedom and adventure. This time has been crystallizing in my mind for several years and it is now, suddenly here—in all its glory!

In just six months, I will be fifty years old and you would have been twenty-one. For some reason, our birthdays loom in my head as a unique occasion that will commemorate a sense of completion—a journey toward mature womanhood and peace. And toward that goal, this past year, I promised myself that I would take proactive strides to fully live my dreams as reality.

A first step came one Sunday afternoon during an excursion through the city. As often happened in those days, a melancholy mood had overshadowed my normally bubbly and effervescent self. It was late on a summer afternoon in August 2000. Feeling stifled in an empty house, I went driving to find something different to satisfy my sense of adventure and to quench my thirst for possibility. My car literally crawled along a road near the mighty Mississippi River on the edges of downtown. I rambled along the rolling river watching the water bubble against the shores. The lush greenery along the blue sky formed a majestic backdrop that soothed my soul. I have always loved water and I have lived near oceans and on lakes many times. But the river brought a different sensation with it. There was movement forward—a symbolic sense of adventure. I really wasn't sure where I was going, but when I came upon a residential complex of Bostonian looking houses, a burst of curious excitement pushed me out of the car and into the model unit of an exquisite new development.

One step inside the model townhouse, I knew that I had found my future home. As the sun streamed through the spacious windows, I explored each floor of the multi-level dwelling. The kitchen was breathtakingly beautiful with its glowing wood floors, granite countertops, handsome cabinetry, and an openness that invited guests to celebrate being together. The living room and dining room were more formal, which I liked. They embodied luxury and elegance with their high ceilings, picturesque large windows, and marble fireplace. The main floor wrapped itself in comfort and a tranquil beauty.

The upstairs layout was perfect! I envisioned myself in the exquisite master bedroom with glorious oversized master bath. There was room for a king-sized bed as well as a cozy sitting area for my antique furniture. The guest room would be perfect for Bess with its private bath and walk-in closet. Excitement tingled through me as I crept downstairs to the hidden lower level only to discover a cozy family room nestled against windows with a view of the entire Minneapolis skyline.

As my eyes devoured the splendor of the different views, a riverfront filled with mighty bridges and sparkling lights as well as a statuesque city skyline, I knew I had arrived at my next home. For many years I had imagined a townhouse designed just like this one. I often dreamed of a personal space that would represent my emancipation and sense of freedom when my family nest was empty.

The townhouse was perfect! I felt as if the whole place was wrapped in a personal package of possibility meant just for me.

For years I had saved money to be able to decorate and furnish my quintessential home with style and grace and when I signed my check to secure the purchase agreement, I secretly celebrated the tangible confirmation of a dream come true.

My townhouse unit would take a year to build, but the year would be filled with the excitement of planning the design and picking out the perfect furnishings to complement my private palace. The timing was perfect since Bess had a year of high school left to finish and I had promised her I wouldn't move until she graduated. Downsizing from a large home of fifteen years of family living would take thoughtful planning and time, but each activity associated with the move represented a cleansing and calming sense of completion of a phase of my life.

By my forty-ninth birthday in February, the townhouse planning was complete and my thoughts turned to other ways to fulfill my dreams. While still employed at the e-commerce company and networking to find a different opportunity, I met a woman who helped put a new plan in place. Lisa was a "life coach" who supported her clients in defining their dreams. She then held them accountable for taking steps toward fulfillment. I was a model client, and within a month I had written a six-month career plan, enrolled in a series of coaching seminars to receive my own training as a personal coach, and I quit my job.

From February to July, I flourished emotionally with a sense of anticipation and freedom. The time off from a full-time job allowed me the opportunity to visit the townhouse and watch its construction on a daily basis. Each time I walked into the new home on the river, I felt a joyful glow. The peaceful feelings I experienced at the townhouse spilled over into my career planning and business development. During this time, I crystallized and implemented the first stages of my new professional vision. I worked diligently on my coach's training, marketing my new business and coaching my first clients. I loved the role of helping others formulate their own dreams and found that I was effective in supporting their needs. I named my coaching/consulting company "Sentient Solutions." The word "sentient" means awareness or "of the senses" (conscious), and it symbolized that I was using both my intellect and intuition to create awareness in others and myself. A sentient being is intuitive, perceptive, insightful, and aware—all the things I wanted to be in my state of fulfillment and well-being. There was a reminiscent familiarity to my Tarot Card reading business, but this time I complemented my intuitive skills with professional training to better serve my clients.

Aside from the coaching practice, there was also lots of time to work on my journal and letters to you, Jill, and I finally drafted the preliminary plan for writing a book to commemorate the twenty-one years since your birth. Additionally, I wanted to utilize my passion for and experience with mentoring, coaching, and personal growth in other ways. I remembered how I loved the opportunity to speak at national conferences when I was an executive with the mentoring company, and so I developed a seminar for women on the value of mentoring and coaching to maximize their potential. I began networking for a venue in which to share my experiences.

The past year, my career vision has crystallized into a trilogy of my passions. Becoming an author, motivational speaking, and life coaching form the heart of that vision. However, the dream of being self-employed will have to be on hold for now. While marketing my coaching business, I was recruited to a national company based here in Minnesota. I will join a new team of national sales executives that specializes in strategic employee recognition programs. I will be selling to Fortune 500 companies on the West Coast. The opportunity is very exciting, despite the fact that it will postpone my plans for entrepreneurship. However, recognition of individuals falls well within the realm of my philosophy on how to value employees as individuals. I am sure that the experience will enrich my life and help develop a broader foundation from which I can speak and coach others.

So, my darling Jill, a lot is happening right now. Yes, it would have been my thirtieth wedding anniversary today, but had I stayed married, there would have been little room for self-exploration and personal adventure. Within the next month I will embark on a whole new phase of life as a single woman whose children have all flown from the nest with liberated wings. I will take Bess to college in Boston, and will return to finalize the purchase of my new town home. The move is planned for the Labor Day weekend and I will start my new job a week after that.

I am gloriously content with my life as it presents itself today. I am also fervently awaiting my passage into the future. Jill, each chapter of our lives brings with it lessons and gifts. I have come to realize that we never stop our process of learning. Sometimes we are called upon to utilize previous lessons to get us through the tough times, but no matter what life brings, there are always gifts associated with the experience and the journey.

∞ DECEMBER 31, 2001

My Dear Jill:

I am nestled by the fireplace in my townhouse with a gorgeous view of the Minneapolis skyline outside my big picture window. Moments ago I watched a spectacular array of fireworks that welcomed in the New Year. As in the past, I have been sitting here reflecting on life. This year I feel differently. Yes, New Year's Eve is always a time for reflection, but tonight my inner thoughts come from a much deeper place than before.

I am wrapped in the solitude of my glorious townhouse with scented candles glimmering against my glass of wine. I am listening to the harmonious sounds of a Kenny G saxophone recording on my overhead audio system and my two precious Shih Tzu puppies have snuggled their warm furry bodies up close to me. However, with sweetness and peaceful images surrounding me, my thoughts drift far away from this setting.

My dearest Jill, a few days after I moved into this luxurious compound, awaiting the start of my lucrative new job, terrorists attacked the United States of America on our homeland. On September 11, 2001, I watched the screen of my new, oversized, precision color television in horror and disbelief as foreign hijackers flew American planes into the New York World Trade Center killing thousands of people. The images were astonishing, heart wrenching and most likely, long lasting.

There was a huge physical disconnect for those of us living in opulent surroundings many states away as we were removed from the immediate danger and seemingly untouched by the trauma. In the days that followed the attacks, we were mystified and distraught over the fact that our strong nation, once thought invincible, could have allowed this to happen. With the suspected villain still at large, there appeared to be no simple resolution and we went about our daily business in spite of the immense destruction that had hit our country and brethren.

The after-effects of what we now call "9/11" are still undetermined. The country's morale suffered and insecurity proliferated amongst people who were normally content with their lives. The economy suffered and America was pushed deeper into an economic recession. Many, many people lost their jobs. I, too, got laid off and in a quirky sort of way, I felt more American.

So often in the past I have written to you, Jill, on the eve of New Year's Day to describe my own quest for fulfillment and peace. This year I must take the rumination beyond my own spiritual and personal development. This year, more than any other, I long for world peace and the assurance that my children and I will be free to live as we have always done.

Life, in its purest form, is the gift for which I am most thankful. We no longer live in a state of blind oblivion ignoring the dangers and threats beyond our grasp. Simplicity replaces opulence as the measure of what we appreciate. Given the state of world politics and terrorism, we must re-think our values and priorities. There may be no tomorrow and we may not be able to live out all of our dreams, so we must enjoy each moment of the present to maximize the gift of life.

I don't know what the New Year will bring in terms of my life. Economic and job security seem like small peas in a pod of insecurity. Will our terrorist attacker be stopped before he mutilates more lives? Will greed and the hunger for powerful control revolutionize our existence and cause freedom to become extinct? These are questions that seem so much more important and powerful than my normal whimsical ponderings on the eve of a new year.

In light of recent world developments, I have adapted some of my core beliefs. I still believe in doing the best that I can to live each day to the fullest. But now, I am more determined to discover ways to give back to others and to the community. I want desperately to reach the point where my unquenchable thirst for personal fulfillment has been met and my abundant energy is passionately devoted to helping someone else. Life is a compilation of days that we live through. Discovery, growth, trepidation, and perseverance are all bundled into the energy of a human being moving forward in their life. It is with reverence that I now fully "trust the Universe" for there must be a power greater than not only I, but greater than the inadequate human beings vying for world leadership.

Jill, my memoir to you thus far recounts my personal struggles, but in the grand scheme of things, those challenges are minute in comparison to a world torn apart by greed and chaos. I am still sitting here, alone, on New Year's Eve, hoping and praying that the next year of my life will bring greater fulfillment and balance. But now those dreams are couched within the perspective of humanity's survival.

My darling, Jill, if you were alive today, you might be here right now sharing this philosophical moment with me by the fire. But in your absence I must send you my thoughts and dreams in these life letters. I haven't given up the quest for personal peace, but the world situation has diminished its singular importance. I maintain that each of us must do what we can to live our lives in harmony with our values. In so doing, I believe that goodness will prevail.

As the dawn breaks tomorrow morning, I will awaken with an excitement that refreshes my spirit and joyfully recasts me on my New Year's path. To live with any less exuberance would be a defeatist's posture. I will still yearn for my dreams to become reality, but within the context of safety and humanity for all people. The goal of living in the present moment and appreciating all that life has to offer will be even more important as I reach my goals of personal emancipation.

Suddenly, I am more inclined to accept my innate qualities as far more important than the accomplishments I achieve. No longer does it matter what job I have, what title I assume, or how much money I make in the course of my career pursuit. Moving forward with a sense of growth, genuine appreciation for learning, and living consistently within my value's system will take precedence over material or financial accomplishments.

I am almost fifty years old, and slowly learning what it means to be "rich." Jill, there is a richness in life that has to do with purity and integrity. As people, I believe we all have similar core ideologies. There is a basic need to be loved and accepted but beyond that we make the richness of our lives with our own choices.

As I have said to you many times in my letters, I strive to develop as a loving and giving individual. I am compelled to utilize and stretch my natural talents to enjoy the by-products of creativity and resourcefulness. I work hard to center within myself a feeling of acceptance so that I may nourish the needs of those I love. Giving is the ultimate prerequisite for receiving.

Jill, I feel so prophetic in my disclosures to you tonight. The 2002 New Year will define more of my story. In the meantime, I will nurture my dreams and anticipate the joyous celebration of "our" coming of age next year. Happy New Year, little one, and bless you for listening and for being there for me tonight.

⌒ APRIL 3, 2002

My Dearest Jill:

Today is your twenty-first birthday. The age of emancipation. Twenty-one marks the true commencement of adulthood and the dawn of womanhood for a young female. Twenty-one is generally an age when the future stands before us as a pure canvas waiting to be painted with the vibrant colors of one's life experiences. Usually it all lies ahead.

But, my darling Jill, your birthday holds a very different meaning for me. These twenty-one years since your birth have been a lifetime unto themselves. The years since you were born have unfolded into a journey of remarkable growth, self-discovery, passionate learning, and love. There has been exceptional achievement and true metamorphosis.

Your twenty-first birthday brings me full circle to an end of a story rather than to the cusp of a new one. This is my story, Jill. Your birth and life helped create my own. I am firmly convinced that giving birth to you, caring for you, and loving you the way I did cast me on a new path. It was through knowing you that life was breathed into my own existence. Your birth was the catalyst that spawned my own development and independence. The journals and letters I have kept over the past twenty-one years have chronicled lessons of intimacy, career exploration, transformation, empowerment, and love...all difficult assignments set before an already grown woman to embrace and explore. The journey has been recorded as if I could pass it back to you, my daughter, to teach you the normal lessons of life and of growing up.

Whenever I have told your story it has become inextricably linked with mine. I feel a deep sense of gratitude each time I speak of the unconditional love and memories of you. The quicksand of time has pulled most of the pain and sadness far from my conscious. What remains, instead, is the sense of joy that your life has had a true purpose—a significance more powerful than most. Jill, I am so grateful for the gift of you.

Today began with tears and a despondent feeling of loss. There was emptiness as I methodically moved through the normal motions of my day. There was a sense of ritual in celebrating "your" day. I wore pink. I do that to commemorate that you were always dressed in pink to contrast with your skin tone as a "blue baby." I carried your picture to work and glanced at your delicate beauty more times than not. I bought my traditional pink rose to honor you. This year, I purchased three delicate pink roses and baby's breath signifying the two plus one of twenty-one.

Ali and Tony went out for dinner with me as a remembrance to your life. Bess called from school in Boston, and in many ways I felt sorry for her that she never met you or had the chance to be a part of your life. This year especially, I kept imagining my two young beauties as soul sisters at ages nineteen and twenty-one. There was a deep sense of wonder all day as to what it might have been like had you lived.

In the course of my day at work, my mind fluttered backward and forward with memories of the past and thoughts about the future. I have kept this journal alive to bring you with me in my journey and to commemorate the gift that you bestowed upon me with your ephemeral life. Some moments, it doesn't really seem like all that much time has passed. What hasn't changed is the depth of feeling for what we shared and the ever-present belief that your life had a purpose and a special meaning.

I still miss you every time someone asks me how many children I have and I stumble silently on the answer. I know that Bess still struggles with the obscure connection to a sister she has never met. When we visit your grave, she points out to me that if we cover up the letters "JILL" on your head stone, we are left with the words "ELIZABETH DAVIS." For her, it is an eerie reminder of the circumstances surrounding her own birth. For me, it is a connection the two of you will always share, even though you have never met.

Bess is in her first year of college at an all girls' school right in the city of Boston. She doesn't love the school or being away from her home city, so she is planning to transfer next year to a local college. Bess has developed into a stunning young woman. She is at a time of her life when her inner thoughts and self-confidence seem to be going through a realignment. While I love her dearly, and am assured she has the most spectacular qualities for success, I sometimes feel incapable of helping her find her true path in life. I am probably being overprotective and in some ways unwilling to let her fly solo from the nest.

When Bess was born so many years after Ali and Tony, and when I got divorced, I secretly wished for the two of us to form a lifelong special bond as mother and daughter as well as friends. At nineteen years old, she is on the cusp of defining her womanhood. Sometimes when she calls me to share her challenges, desires, and personal ideas, I am mesmerized by her intelligence, strength, and clarity. She is growing up *her way*, independent of my constant companionship or guidance. That, alone, makes her a stronger woman than I was at that age. She has already absorbed the wisdom from my experiences and she has the constant love and support of her brother and sister. Bess is a vibrant young woman with an astonishing outer beauty that is complemented by extraordinary God-given talents of intelligence, tenacity, strong personal resolve, and fearless energy.

As with Maslow's hierarchy, I am confident that as Bess continues in her pursuit of a life direction, and her significant relationships fall into place, she will complement her tremendous self-focus with a generosity and caring nature. For now, she needs to fulfill her own sense of security before she can branch out toward others. My love for Bess is unique.

After your death, Bess was a joyous gift in my life. She was never a replacement for you, for I never believed I would have another daughter after you died. Elizabeth Anne's birth brought with it a supplemental joy to a family fraught with sorrow and grief. Her mere existence continues to be a miraculous breath of fresh air to all who know her. She is like a glorious gust of wind that whips into your life and whirls you around in a myriad of emotions.

Each day, as I become more centered in my life, I recognize the future belongs to my children. Not only do they have their entire adult life before them, but also, they will provide many of the rewards of my elder years. Their growth, emancipation, and maturity will lead to lasting relationships and new loves. Their happiness will give me a different sense of peace.

Of all my children, Ali is the closest to completing that journey on her own. When I look at my four children's baby pictures on my bedroom wall, I see the physical similarity that you had to your sister Ali. I often wonder how you might have resembled her as a grown woman and what your relationship would have been like. Ali is silent in her thoughts, but I am assured your memory holds a special place in her heart.

Ali is an elementary school teacher—her love of children has never diminished. She is blessed with maternal qualities of caring and compassion. She has been an older sister (helping to raise Bess as a primary caregiver), a full-time nanny, and a teacher. I cherish the hope that she will one day be blessed with a child of her own. Ali is in a wonderful relationship; she recently became engaged to Nathan, her boyfriend of two-and-a-half years. She met Nathan at the elementary school where she teaches. Their relationship appears to be solidly built from time spent as colleagues, friends, and then lovers. Nathan is also raising his two beautiful daughters and I marvel at the patience, creativity, and compassion he has for his children. Mostly, however, I love to watch Ali and Nathan together. They share so much between them, it is visible in their eyes and in the way they silently communicate with each other. He appears to adore her, and she loves him and his children—that's very evident. I am eager for her to experience the joy of childbirth and motherhood—for it is the greatest joy I have ever known. I know that she will be an exceptionally capable and loving mother.

Tony has grown into a masculine, yet caring, six-foot tall man. He is still strong-willed and sensitive, but he has matured into a person of character and depth. You continue to hold a very special place in his heart and memory. He never misses your birthday or the anniversary of your death without a visit to the cemetery. In his mind, he still has three sisters, although one of them has been absent from his life for twenty years. He graduated with a double-English major from Creighton University in Omaha, Nebraska, a few years ago. While he was there, he wrote extensively. He won the University's nonfiction writing award and his senior thesis, a compilation of his own creative writing, was stellar. Of course, there was an astonishingly beautiful tribute to you among the entries.

Tony has chosen the restaurant industry as his profession. He has an extraordinary passion for people and relationship building and he loves the "art of fine dining" (an interest he may have picked up from his mom who has always been totally preoccupied and in love with food and wine!). He has worked for the past three years as a manager of the city's top restaurant corporation. Although he works very long hours, he is content and growing in responsibility, maturity, and the enjoyment of his life. He loves his personal interaction with restaurant customers and everywhere I go people compliment me on the generous, charismatic young man I have raised.

And, yes, he still has the "Tony spark" that I treasure. Just yesterday he came over to my house and delivered a bouquet of flowers for no special reason! Despite the adversity of his early years, his sensitivity and loving spirit prevail. I am so proud of his perseverance, his compassion, and his giving heart. I am proud of all three children who remain constant blessings in my life.

Many years ago I discovered a wonderful quote by Sophocles that says: "Children are the anchors that hold a mother to life." How very true that is.

And you, my darling Jill, are the anchor that ties me to my spirituality and to the meaning of life. Today, your twenty-first birthday memorializes my own growth and journey since your birth. It also commemorates a spiritual passage toward peace and a commencement of the final chapter in the memoirs of a woman.

For years now I have written to you to describe how your existence impacted my growth as a woman. Throughout my journal you are remembered and revered for your role in my development. Your life and death is a constant reminder that there are gifts in life from which we can learn. The symbolism of today, what would have been your twenty-first birthday, is inextricably linked with my own coming of age.

Since your death, I have actively pursued an emotional quest for independence. I followed the doctrine that "life is a journey and an exploration of our potential." In the course of my pursuit, I studied metaphysics and participated in several empowerment workshops that utilized meditation and personal affirmations to turn dreams into reality. I aligned myself with the spiritual belief that "if you can dream it, you can achieve it," and I actively practiced my new faith.

As I experienced and emerged from your death, I learned that grief is an elusive concept with a complex character. Grief has multiple personalities like the humanity it invades. But, despite all its torment and sorrow, grief has a redeeming virtue. With the right light shining upon it, we can see the illumination of dawn in the darkest moments. When accepted as a gift, grief spawns growth.

It took me almost twenty-one years to fully appreciate the value of this gift and to uniformly apply it to other aspects of my life. It was then that I knew this book had to be written and shared with others. In doing so, it validated my "gift philosophy" and immortalized my belief that you, my daughter, served a divine purpose.

My book promotes the belief that an intrinsic reward can be found in everything that happens to us. The story demonstrates that through adversity and the challenges I faced in both my personal and professional life, I learned to trust the power of the universe. I have learned that there is a divine wisdom for that which happens to us. Although we may not always know the reason why we are given difficult challenges, if we learn to accept them as "gifts" we are able to live more as empowered beings rather than as victims of our own circumstances.

While I have completed this memoir, I know the journey is not complete. I am still working toward completion of a lifelong dream: to become a successful entrepreneur and independent businesswoman. My goal is to consult with companies and individuals on development and maximizing human potential. Through motivational speaking engagements and private coaching consultations, I want to share what I have learned—that there are gifts in adversity.

I have found a sense of peace in my life as a single woman. I often embrace solitude as if it were a thermal cloak of safety warming my soul. I love my home life and the unconditional love of my precious pups. I am grateful for the joys of family and friends. While I don't have a romantic relationship right now, I am content. I hold onto my conviction that when the right love comes along it will be a gift.

I am also appreciative for the opportunity to volunteer once again at your Children's Hospital. I am currently helping to raise funds for a new heart catheterization laboratory that will specifically serve infants and children. And early next year, I will begin a new term as a board member of the Children's Hospital Foundation. I have always said, my heart remains at Children's. For when I am there, I feel closer to you.

Your memory will always transcend my existence. My memoir will be my lasting tribute to your life. It is written in hopes that it forms the capstone of my development. My passion for personal development reaches beyond my love of writing and the creation of my memoir. By writing *The Heart's Gift* I wanted to honor the principle of giving.

While I have written these cherished letters to you, Jill, I am also offering readers my personal story and the memories that sparked my own learning. I want my readers to intimately wander the pathway with me. I want the people who read my book to find comfort in their own quest and to reach for their own stars. I have written a memoir that I hope becomes a legacy for learning.

My darling Jill, you have provided me with a magnificent journey. I have been blessed with the gift of you. Your spirit lives on in my heart and your presence nourishes my soul. I will always love you.

Thank you, Jill. You have given me the gift of life.